The Twentieth Century

John D Clare

Contents

Nelson

THE CAUSES OF THE FIRST WORLD WAR

Europe in 1914

In 1914, Germany had only two allies (friends): Austria-Hungary and weak, unreliable Italy. These three countries had formed an alliance called the Triple Alliance.

Other countries, however, were hostile towards Germany. France, Russia and Great Britain had joined themselves into the 'Triple Entente' – an alliance against Germany. Serbia was Russia's ally. Japan had made an alliance with Great Britain. Germans felt that they were surrounded by enemies.

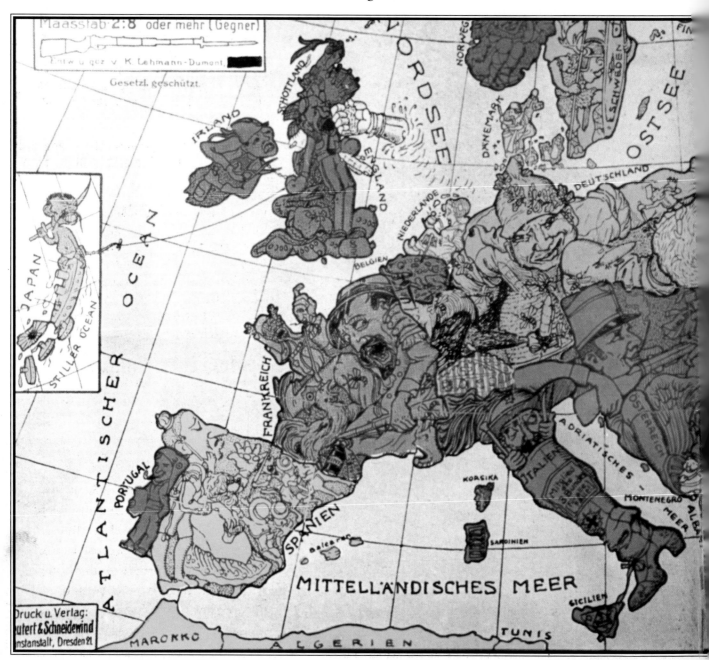

This German cartoon-map of 1914 shows 'Germany under threat from its enemies'. The map shows the political boundaries fairly accurately. It is possible to see how different they were from today's national boundaries – particularly in central and eastern Europe.

The scale, which is shown in the shape of a rifle, translates as: 'Scale: 2 to 8 or more (enemies)'.

Österreich Ungarn	Austria-Hungary
Serbien	Serbia
Deutschland	Germany
Russland	Russia
Frankreich	France
Griechenland	Greece
Mittelländisches Meer	Mediterranean
Schwarzes Meer	Black Sea
Ostsee	Baltic Sea
Stiller Ocean	Pacific Ocean
Marokko	Morocco

⁇ QUESTIONS ⁇

1 Look at the faces of Austria-Hungary and Germany. Were the Germans afraid of their enemies ranged against them?

2 Look at the faces of Britain, France and Russia. Which country was Germany most afraid of? How can you tell?

The Long-term Causes of the First World War

The causes of the War went back long before 1914. It only needed a tiny spark to set all Europe at war. Historians suggest that there were four 'long-term' causes of 5 the First World War.

1 Nationalism

The most important of these pressures was **nationalism**. This means thinking your country is better than others (*see page 5*). This caused hatred and rivalry between 10 countries.

2 Imperialism

Nations who thought that they were greater than others felt they had the right to rule over others. So nationalism led to **imperialism** – the desire to conquer other 15 lands and to build an empire. The European nations had conquered most of the rest of the world. The countries they owned were called *colonies*. Imperialism often caused conflict between the nations 20 of Europe.

3 Militarism

This was a race to build the greatest armies and navies. It was another result of nationalism. Each nation was afraid of the others, and wanted to be able to defend 35 itself. The nations of Europe built up huge armed forces (*see table, below*). By 1914, they were ready for war; all that was needed was something to start them fighting.

4 Alliances

Meanwhile, the countries of Europe formed 40 themselves into two hostile **alliances**, the Triple Entente (France, Russia and Great Britain) and the Triple Alliance (Germany, Austria-Hungary and Italy). The system of alliances encouraged nations to be more 45 aggressive. This was because they knew they could rely on the help of friends if there was a war. Like mountain climbers tied to the same rope, it pulled them into war when the crisis came. 50

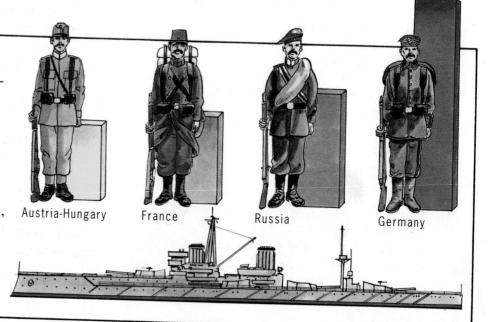

Size of armed forces In 1914

Germany	8.5 million
Russia	4.4 million
France	3.5 million
Austria-Hungary	3 million

25 Although the British Expeditionary Force was only 711,000 strong, the British navy insisted on being as large as the 30 other powers' navies put together.

Austria-Hungary   France   Russia   Germany

Nationalism

The most important long-term cause of the war was nationalism. The sources on this page will help you to understand nationalism in Europe in 1914.

Left: nationalism is an extreme form of patriotism. The Promenade Concerts ('The Proms') were founded by Sir Henry Wood in 1895. Even today, on the *Last Night of the Proms*, audiences wave British flags and sing along to music that glorifies Great Britain. 80

In 1914, Germany's unofficial 'national anthem' was: 85

Deutschland über Alles
Germany, Germany over all,
  over everything else in the world,
When it steadfastly holds together,
  offensively and defensively, 90
  with brotherhood . . .

1 The French boasted about their national *élan* (spirit).
The Marseillaise became France's national anthem in 1879.
55 The French hated the Germans, who had defeated them in the war of 1870–1. The sixth verse runs:

The Marseillaise
Sacred love of the Fatherland,
Guide and support our vengeful arms.
60 Liberty, beloved liberty,
Fight with your defenders (*repeat*)
Under our flags so that victory will rush
  to your manly strains;
That your dying enemies shall see your
65   triumph and glory!

  To Arms, citizens! Form your battalions,
  Let us march, let us march!
  That their impure blood should water
  our fields.

70 **liberty**: freedom

2 Although Germany had become a united country only in 1871, the Germans were proud of their *Technik* (science and efficiency) and *Kultur* (art, history and way of life). Germany 75 was also Britain's great rival for trade.

3 The British did not think they were the greatest nation on earth – they *knew* it! British music hall audiences sang these songs: 95

Land of Hope and Glory
Land of hope and glory, mother of
  the free.
How shall we extol thee, who are born
  of thee?
Wider still and wider shall thy bounds 100
  be set;
God, who made thee mighty, make
  thee mightier yet (*repeat*)

extol: say good things about, praise
bounds: national boundaries 105

Rule Britannia
Rule Britannia! Britannia rule the waves;
Britons never, never, never shall be
  slaves.

5

Events leading up to the First World War

1870-1 The German Empire
Germany became a united country. German forces defeated France. The French had to give up the provinces of Alsace and Lorraine. They wanted revenge.

1878 Treaty of San Stefano
Serbia became an independent country. The Serbs were very nationalistic. They wanted to unite the Serbs into one country.

1898 Fashoda incident
English and French forces clashed in the Sudan, almost causing a war.

1899-1902 Boer War
Britain defeated the Boer rebels in South Africa. Kaiser Wilhelm said he supported the Boers. Britain was angry with Germany.

1900 Second German Navy Law
Germany planned to increase the German Navy to 38 battleships.

1902 Anglo-Japanese Treaty
Britain came to a naval agreement with Japan.

1903 Berlin-Baghdad Railway
France and Britain objected to Germany's plans for a railway from Berlin to Baghdad in the Turkish Empire. They feared that Germany was trying to get control over Turkey.

1904 Anglo-French Entente Cordiale
A 'friendly agreement' between Britain and France.

1904-1905 Russo-Japanese War
When Japan defeated the Russians, people realised that Russia was militarily weak.

1906 HMS Dreadnought
The first Dreadnought warship was launched in Britain.

1907 Entente between Britain and Russia
An agreement between Britain and Russia.

1908 Bosnia
Austria-Hungary annexed (took over) Bosnia from the Turks.

1908 Daily Telegraph Article
In a *Daily Telegraph* interview, Kaiser Wilhelm said that the German people disliked Britain, but he liked Britain. The British people were angry.

1911 Agadir Crisis
Germany sent a gunboat, *The Panther*, to the Moroccan port of Agadir. Kaiser Wilhelm demanded a 'place in the sun' for Germany. France and Britain prepared for war. Germany backed down.

1912–1913 Balkan Wars
Turkey was almost driven out of the Balkans (south-east Europe). The Serbian Prime Minister, warned, 'The first round is won. Now for the second round – against Austria'.

Murder at Sarajevo

The First World War began with an assassination (a political murder). These pictures tell the story of the 'spark' that started the war.

1 The city of Sarajevo in 1914. The main road – the Appel Quay – can be clearly seen next to the river. Sarajevo was the capital of the province of Bosnia, in Austria-Hungary. Many Serbs lived in Bosnia. A group nicknamed the 'Black Hand' wanted Bosnia to be part of Serbia. They started a terrorist war against the Austrians, with bombings and shootings.

2 On 28 June 1914, Franz Ferdinand (the heir to the throne of Austria-Hungary) and his wife Sophie visited Sarajevo. They arrived at the station at 9.28 am (*above*). It was Franz Ferdinand's wedding anniversary. It was also Serbia's National Day. Lined up along the Appel Quay, waiting for the Archduke, were six young men. They were going to try to murder Franz Ferdinand.

3 The Archduke's motorcade drove along the Appel Quay. Four of the young men did nothing. But one threw a bomb. It missed. The motorcade sped to the Town Hall and the Archduke was safe. He decided to go home immediately, by a different route. At 11 am, the Archduke and his wife left the Town Hall (*above*). In the confusion, nobody told the driver of the change of route.

4 The car started back along the Appel Quay, but then the driver went the wrong way. He was told to turn round. By chance, he stopped the car in front of one of the assassins, Gavrilo Princip. Princip fired two shots. The first hit the Archduke's throat. The second hit Sophie in the stomach. They both died almost immediately. It was 11.30 am. Princip was arrested and beaten up (*above*).

Five Steps to World War

1 Austria declares war

Austria-Hungary was a world power, but it was afraid of Serbia. Many different races lived in the Austro-Hungarian empire and fifteen different languages were spoken within its borders. If nationalism became popular in Austria-Hungary, the empire would fall apart. Many people in Austria-Hungary wanted to attack Serbia to destroy the Black Hand and 'teach the nationalists a lesson'. Franz Ferdinand had not been very popular in Austria. But his murder gave Austrian politicians the opportunity to get tough with the Serbs. On 23 July 1914, they sent Serbia ten demands. Serbia, they said, must meet all these demands, or they would declare war (this is called an **ultimatum**).

The Austrians made the terms of the ultimatum very harsh. They hoped the Serbs would have to refuse them, and then Austria-Hungary would have an excuse to invade Serbia.

The Serbs accepted all the points but one. So, on 28 July, Austria declared war on Serbia. The Austrian government, however, had been wrong-footed by the Serbs. The Austrian declaration of war looked unreasonable and unfair. Serbia called up her army and asked her ally, Russia, for help.

2 Russia mobilises

The Russians debated what to do. They knew that Russia was too weak to go to war. However, they did not want to let Serbia down. For Tsar Nicholas, the ruler of Russia, it was a matter of right and wrong. 'An unjust war has been declared on a weak country,' he said. On 31 July 1914, he mobilised (called up) the Russian army.

Apart from Britain, all the countries of Europe had vast armies. Most of their soldiers were 'reservists' – trained soldiers who lived at home, but were ready to be mobilised if there was a war. In this picture German soldiers board the train which will take them to their units. The slogans they have chalked on the carriages say things like, 'Excursion to Paris', 'Goodbye to the Boulevard', 'I'm itching to use my sword-point in this struggle.'

3 Germany attacks

Germany was Austria's ally. The Russian mobilisation threw the Germans into a panic. They had expected a war against
60 France and Russia. They had expected the Russian Army to take a long time to mobilise. The German plan – the 'Schlieffen Plan' – was to march through Belgium, conquer France quickly, and then turn back
65 to face the Russian army. Now the plan was going wrong. Russia was mobilising first, and was going to be ready too soon!

Also, German politicians feared Russia. Russia was weak, but was growing stronger
70 all the time. 1914 was a good time for a war, before Russia got too strong. 'We are ready . . . and the sooner the better for us,' the German General von Moltke said. On 1 August 1914, Germany declared war on
75 Russia. Two days later Germany declared war on France and the German army marched into Belgium.

4 France fights back

Germany attacked France in 1914, but the French were ready and eager for a fight. Enthusiastic crowds gathered in Paris to 80 cheer the soldiers off to war.

5 Britain joins in

In a treaty of 1839, Britain had promised to defend Belgium if it was invaded. So, on 4 August, the British government sent an ultimatum to the Germans demanding 85 that they promise to withdraw their troops immediately. The German ministers were angry and amazed that Britain would consider going to war 'for a scrap of paper', but they could not call back their 90 army.

'Like a line of falling dominoes,' one historian has written, 'the nations of Europe toppled each other over into war.'

The deadline for 95 Germany to accept Britain's ultimatum was midnight (11 pm British time) on 4 August 1914. It was a beautiful 100 summer's day. All over Europe cheering crowds sang patriotic songs and waved flags. At 11 pm the deadline 105 passed. Germany had ignored the British ultimatum. The crowds in Parliament Square in London turned and ran 110 home in all directions. As they ran, they shouted, 'War! War! War!'

9

THE FIRST WORLD WAR

The Ultimate Sacrifice

In the 1960s, when I was your age, a man used to come round door-to-door selling brushes. It was impossible to understand what he said. He just opened an old brown suitcase and pointed. I hated meeting him. Every one of his limbs twitched violently; no part of his body was ever still. Day and night, he shook all over. He had shell-shock. His nerves had been shattered in the First World War, and he had lived in that condition for fifty years. We always bought something from him, because we felt sorry for him. He had not died in the War, but he had given his life for his country.

Both the poems on these pages look at the idea of giving your life for your country.

A man with shell shock. An advanced dressing station at Ypres, 1917.

The Soldier   *Rupert Brooke*

If I should die, think only this of me:
That there's some corner of a foreign field
That is for ever England. There shall be
In that rich earth a richer dust concealed;
5 A dust whom England bore, shaped and made aware,
Gave, once, her flowers to love, her ways to roam,
A body of England's breathing English air,
Washed by the rivers, blest by suns of home.

And think, this heart, all evil shed away,
10 A pulse in the eternal mind, no less
Gives somewhere back the thoughts by England given;
Her sights and sounds; dreams happy as her day;
And laughter, learnt of friends; and gentleness,
In hearts at peace, under an English heaven.

Poppy fields. Poppies were one of the few flowers which grew on the battlefields of the First World War in France.

Ever since, they have been a symbol of remembrance for those who died.

A gas attack. Notice the different gas masks the soldiers are wearing.

Dulce et Decorum Est   *Wilfred Owen*

This poem tells the story of a phosgene gas attack as troops were making their way back from the front line.
The Latin saying *Dulce et decorum est pro patria mori* means:
'It is sweet and noble to die for your country'.

Bent double, like old beggars under sacks,
Knock-kneed, coughing like hags, we cursed through sludge,
Till on the haunting flares we turned our backs,
And towards our distant rest began to trudge.
5 Men marched asleep. Many had lost their boots,
But limped on, blood-shod. All went lame; all blind;
Drunk with fatigue; deaf even to the hoots
Of gas-shells dropping softly behind.

Gas! Gas! Quick boys – An ecstasy of fumbling,
10 Fitting the clumsy helmets just in time;
But someone still was yelling out and stumbling
And floundering like a man in fire or lime –
Dim, through the misty panes and thick green light,
As under a green sea, I saw him drowning.
15 In all my dreams, before my helpless sight,
He plunges at me, guttering, choking, drowning.

If in some smothering dreams, you too could pace
Behind the wagon that we flung him in,
And watch the white eyes writhing in his face,
20 His hanging face, like a devil's sick of sin;
If you could hear, at every jolt, the blood
Come gurgling from the froth-corrupted lungs,
Obscene as cancer, bitter as the cud
Of vile, incurable sores on innocent tongues –
25 My friend, you would not tell with such high zest
To children ardent for some desperate glory,
The old Lie: *Dulce et decorum est*
Pro patria mori.

? ? ? ? ? QUESTIONS ? ? ? ? ?

1 In what ways are the two poems different?
2 What do the authors feel about England, the War, and death?
3 Which poem, do you think, was written first?

1

The First World War

The Western Front

The First World War was the first world war. Fighting took place all over the world (*see map, page 13*). Troops from Australia, New Zealand, Canada, India, Egypt and
5 the West Indies fought with the British Army. Nevertheless, the most important battles took place in north-eastern France (the 'Western Front').

On 3 August 1914, Germany invaded
10 Belgium. By September 1914, the German Army was only 30 miles from Paris. There, however, at the battle of the Marne, the Germans were stopped. The British and French armies advanced. The Germans dug
15 trenches to defend themselves. The British and French armies were stopped.

At first, as they could no longer go forward, both armies moved sideways. They tried to outflank (get round behind)
20 the other. They dug trenches as they went. They did this until they reached the sea and couldn't go any further. This part of the war is usually called 'the race to the sea' (September–November, 1914). The
25 result was a line of trenches stretching from Switzerland to the English Channel.

Next, both sides tried to break through the enemy's trenches. It was impossible. Men defended with shells and machine guns. They advanced on foot, with rifles. 30
The war became a deadly stalemate.

By 1916, both sides had realised that they would never break the enemy's lines. They decided simply to try to wear out the enemy by killing more men than they lost. 35
Sometimes they attacked in small raids. Sometimes they made huge attacks – as at the battles of Verdun (February–December 1916), the Somme (July–November 1916) and Passchendaele (July–November 1917). 40
Millions of soldiers died trying to capture a few hundred more yards of mud. This is sometimes called the War of Attrition (wearing down).

In April 1915, at the second battle of 45
Ypres, the Germans became the first people to use poison gas in warfare. The British first used the tank as a weapon at the battle of the Somme in September 1916. The motor car and the aeroplane were first 50
used in warfare on the western front. But nothing could break the stalemate.

Left: Tank warfare – the ideal. British troops shelter behind Mark V 55
Tanks during an advance in 1918. In front, the tanks carry 'cribs'. The idea was that, on meeting a deep trench or crater, 60
the tank could drop the crib into the hole and then drive over it safely. Neither the cribs, nor the tanks, worked very well 65
in practice.

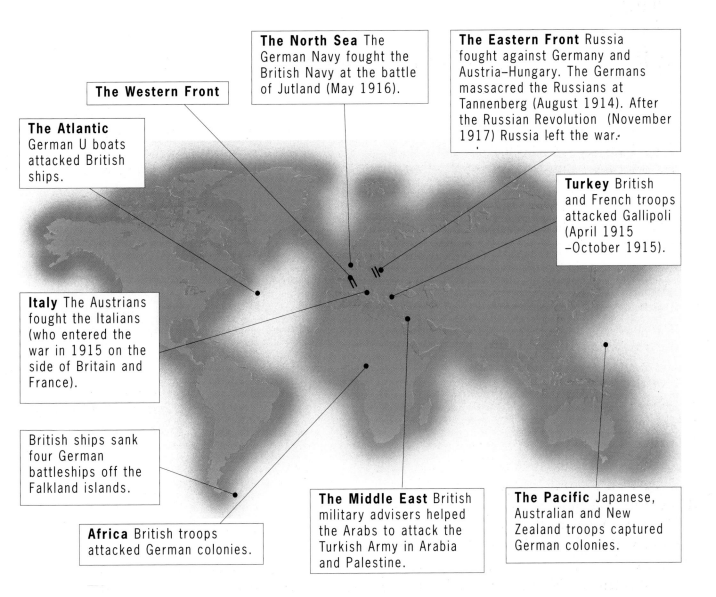

The Western Front

The North Sea The German Navy fought the British Navy at the battle of Jutland (May 1916).

The Eastern Front Russia fought against Germany and Austria–Hungary. The Germans massacred the Russians at Tannenberg (August 1914). After the Russian Revolution (November 1917) Russia left the war.

The Atlantic German U boats attacked British ships.

Turkey British and French troops attacked Gallipoli (April 1915 –October 1915).

Italy The Austrians fought the Italians (who entered the war in 1915 on the side of Britain and France).

British ships sank four German battleships off the Falkland islands.

Africa British troops attacked German colonies.

The Middle East British military advisers helped the Arabs to attack the Turkish Army in Arabia and Palestine.

The Pacific Japanese, Australian and New Zealand troops captured German colonies.

Total War

The First World War was the first war to involve whole nations in the fighting. The German Navy shelled Hartlepool,
70 Scarborough and Whitby (December 1914). German Zeppelin airships bombed London.

Women, as well as men, went to war. They joined the armed forces as cooks, carpenters and drivers. They served as
75 nurses on the Western Front. At home, they worked in arms factories, and as firemen, bus drivers and navvies.

Both sides tried to starve the other into defeat. German U-boats sank British
80 merchant ships, and the British navy blockaded German ports. The German

Navy tried to break the blockade at the sea battle of Jutland (May 1916), but failed. By 1918, many Germans were living on potatoes and berries. 85

The end of the War

America entered the war in April 1917. In March 1918, therefore, the Germans launched a huge attack, hoping to gain victory before the American Army could get to France. However, this attack collapsed on 90 8 August 1918. It was the German Army's 'Black Day'. The Germans realised that they were going to be defeated. They signed an armistice (ceasefire), which began at 11 am on 11 November 1918. 95

Join Up!

At the time of the First World War, all the great powers of Europe relied on **conscription**. They 'called up' their men to the army. Only Britain had a voluntary army (Britain did not introduce conscription until 1916, two years after the war started).

The British Commander-in-Chief, Lord Kitchener (*picture 10*) realised that vast numbers of men would be needed.

A huge **propaganda** campaign was therefore mounted to try to persuade men to join up. Posters played a major role in this campaign.

3

YOUR COUNTRY'S CALL

Isn't this worth fighting for?
ENLIST NOW

1

WAR
TO ARMS CITIZENS OF THE EMPIRE!!

2

RED CROSS OR IRON CROSS?

WOUNDED AND A PRISONER OUR SOLDIER CRIES FOR WATER.
THE GERMAN "SISTER" POURS IT ON THE GROUND BEFORE HIS EYES.
THERE IS NO WOMAN IN BRITAIN WHO WOULD DO IT.
THERE IS NO WOMAN IN BRITAIN WHO WILL FORGET IT.

4

Are YOU in this?

5

PUBLIC SCHOOLS BRIGADE
ROYAL FUSILIERS
118th INFANTRY BRIGADE

HURRY UP! BOYS
RECRUITING OFFICE
20, WESTMINSTER PALACE GARDENS
WESTMINSTER, S.W.
FILL THE RANKS

6

FORWARD!

Forward to Victory
ENLIST NOW

7

REMEMBER BELGIUM

ENLIST TO-DAY

8

TO THE
YOUNG WOMEN
OF LONDON

Is your "Best Boy" wearing
Khaki?   If not don't YOU
THINK he should be?

If he does not think that you
and your country are worth
fighting for—do you think he
is WORTHY of you?

Don't pity the girl who is
alone—her young man is
probably a soldier—fighting
for her and her country—
and for YOU.

If your young man neglects his duty to his
King and Country, the time may come when
he will NEGLECT YOU.

Think it over—then ask him to

JOIN THE ARMY TO-DAY

9

Daddy, what did YOU do in the Great War?

10

BRITONS

"WANTS"
YOU

JOIN YOUR COUNTRY'S ARMY!
GOD SAVE THE KING
Reproduced by permission of LONDON OPINION

15

Off to War with the Durham Light Infantry

The following pictures show men from County Durham in England joining up and doing their basic training.

The Western Front in Pictures

The First World War was the first war to be extensively photographed. These have left a powerful record of the fighting, as the pictures on the following pages prove.

No Man's Land during the Battle of Passchendaele, 1917, with **shell craters**. Soldiers who had taken cover in a large dry crater, taunted their comrades in craters such as these by singing a popular soldiers' song: 'I've got a **better 'ole** than you.'

Australian **Artillery** at the Battle of Passchendaele, 1917. The gun is a Mark IV Howitzer. Notice the 8-inch shells in the foreground. Shells were the greatest killer of men in the First World War.

Front line trench of the Second Australian Division in Flanders, 18 May 1916. Look at the **revetments** (walling), the wooden **duckboards** over the mud in the bottom of the trench, and the **firestep** for the soldiers to stand on to fire. The front edge of the trench is called the **parapet**, the back is called the **parados**. The soldier in the right foreground is looking over the parapet using a **periscope**. The soldier in the centre carries a **Lewis gun**.

4a

4b

(Far *left*) The trench system at Moquet Farm. Note the two lines of trenches running north to south, joined by a **communication trench** (north of the farm), running east-west.

(*Left*) The same place after the preliminary bombardment before the battle of the Somme, 1916. The British guns fired over 1.7 million shells in eight days.

British Sopwith Camel Biplanes, 203 Squadron of the RAF.

A German **Fokker E1 monoplane** (single wing). The machine gun fired through the propeller as it turned.

A British **messenger dog** is given its message.

A **sniper**, disguised as a tree, June 1917.

Pumping out the front line, January 1917. The men look quite cheerful. Notice the **sandbags** and the **capes**.

British officers in a captured **dugout**. Note the electric light, the wallpaper and the gramaphone.

20

The British often dug tunnels ('**mines**') under the German lines, which they blew up before attacking. This is one of the mines exploded on the first day of the battle of the Somme, 1 July 1916. It contained 9000 kilos of explosive and blew a hole 40 metres across and 18 metres deep.

A German throws a **stick grenade**, nicknamed a 'potato masher'. Its timed fuse sometimes allowed British troops to throw it back. The British used a **Mills 'shatter' grenade** which exploded when it hit something.

British **machine gun**, 1918.

Tanks were slow, and often got stuck in the mud, or toppled over, as this British tank did on 20 November 1917, during the battle of Passchendaele.

The Hero

This letter was written in 1918 by a young officer named Frank Kelly. He had been wounded during an attack, and Sergeant Harry Clare had carried him back to the British lines. He had, in fact, saved his life.

rally: to encourage the men to continue attacking when they are beginning to lose heart.
get a commission: to be promoted to the rank of officer.
pocket-book: diary. **Tommy** was a popular word for a British soldier.

Sergeant
Harry Clare

Sunderland
April 30th /18

My Dear Sgt Clare,

I was exceedingly pleased to hear from you
5 yesterday. Do you know despite the number
of times you told me your name I could no
more remember it than the man in the moon.
And now my first duty is to try to express
to you my feeling of gratitude for all you did
10 for me on Mar 27th. I fully realise how
different my condition might now be but for
your gallant conduct. Do not think that you
were at all responsible for my wound. It
was my duty to rally the men. Indeed I cannot
15 understand where they got the idea of retiring like that.
I hear you are likely to get to England for a commission.
Needless to say I shall be delighted to see you. There are one
or two things I should like to talk to you about specially. By the
way you may remember when I was hit I gave my pocket-book
20 to a Tommy to return home. I had it returned to me today. Do
you happen to know who the 'Tommy' was? I should like to
send him something.
And now about my present condition. I am still lying almost
flat but the wound is much improved, it having turned out very
25 dirty. I fear when I was hit I proved very childish but I hope you
will forgive me. I really seem to have acted more like a
drunken man than anything else.
Please excuse this ill-written rambling letter. I am sure you
will realise that it is written under difficulties and I cannot well
30 write it again. Write again as soon as you can. I shall always
be pleased to hear from you.

Cheerio. Good luck.
Ever yours sincerely,

Frank Kelly

QUESTION

Work out from the letter the order in which things happened on 27 March.

Night in No Man's Land

The historian Lynn Macdonald has interviewed men who fought on the Western Front the First World War. This man remembers sheltering in craters in No Man's Land, waiting to go 'over the top'.

A British night patrol 'lighting up'.Romantic photographs like these were set up in advance, and taken for propaganda for the people in England.
  Notice the barbed wire.

Most of my boys were young Londoners, just eighteen or nineteen, and a lot of them were going into a fight for the first time. Regularly during the night I crawled round to check on
5 my scattered sections, having a word here and there and trying to keep their spirits up. The stench was horrible, for the bodies were not corpses in the normal sense. With all the shell-fire and bombardments they'd been
10 continually disturbed, and the whole place was a mess of filth and slime and bones and decomposing bits of flesh. Everyone was on edge and as I crawled up to one shell-hole I could hear a boy sobbing and crying. He was
15 crying for his mother. It was pathetic, really, he just kept saying over and over again, "Oh Mum! Oh Mum!"
  Nothing would make him shut up and while it wasn't likely that the Germans could hear, it
20 was quite obvious that when there were lulls in the shell-fire the men in the shell-holes on either side would hear this lad and possibly be affected.
  Depression, even panic, can spread quite
25 easily in a situation like that. So I crawled into the shell-hole and asked Corporal Merton what was going on. He said, "It's his first time in the line, sir, I can't keep him quiet, and he's making the other lads jittery." Well the other
30 boys in the shell-hole obviously *were* jittery

and, as one of them put it more succinctly, "fed up with his bleedin' noise". Then they all joined in, "Send him down the line and home to Mum" – "Give him a clout and knock him out" – "Tell him to put a sock in it, sir." 35
  I tried to reason with the boy, but the more I talked to him the more distraught he became, until he was almost screaming, "I can't stay here! Let me go! I want my mum!" So I switched my tactics, called him a 40 coward, threatened him with court-martial, and when that didn't work I simply pulled him towards me and slapped his face as hard as I could several times. It had an extraordinary effect. There was absolute silence in the shell- 45 hole and then the corporal, who was a much older man, said, "I think I can manage him now, sir." Well he took that boy in his arms, just as if he was a small child and when I crawled back a little later to see if all was 50 well, they were both lying there asleep and the corporal still had his arms round the boy – mud, equipment and all. At zero hour they went over together.

Lieutenant A Angel, *Royal Fusiliers,* 55
38th Division.
Lt. Angel lost an eye in the attack. The boy who had lost his nerve did 'go home to mum' – he was hit and wounded. Corporal Merton was killed in the same burst of machine gun fire which wounded 60 *the boy; he had stayed close to the boy and they had gone together 'over the top'.* **23**

In Battle

Different soldiers reacted to the war in different ways; in these sources, different soldiers describe their feelings during a battle.

1 Julian Grenfell

A young poet, killed on 26 May 1915.

I adore war. It's like a big picnic . . . I've never been so well or happy. No one grumbles at one for being dirty. I have only had my boots off once in the last ten days and only washed twice.

2 Lieutenant J Annan

A soldier in the Royal Scots Regiment.

Uncomfortable, I should say it was. Our kilts were soaking, and when you sit in the freezing cold with a wet kilt between your legs it's beyond description.

There was a lull in the shelling, and we heard this terrible kind of gurgling noise. It was the wounded, lying there sinking, and this liquid mud burying them alive, running over their faces into their mouth and nose . . . We couldn't understand why, in the name of God, anyone had ordered an attack like that over terrain like that. It was impossible.

3 Rifleman E Chapman

The bombardment was sheer hell . . . my pal was hit with a piece of shell which sliced his head completely off. You can imagine how I felt . . . Giving up all hope of survival and feeling hopping mad, I waited with my Lewis gun for the enemy to come over the top.

4 A soldier of the British Machine Gun Corps.

He describes his actions during the battle of the Somme, 1916.

To the south of the wood Germans could be seen, silhouetted against the sky-line, moving forward. I fired at them and watched them fall, chuckling with joy at the technical efficiency of the machine-gun . . . Anger, and the intensity of the fire, consumed my spirit and not caring for the consequences, I rose and turned my machine gun upon them, laughing loudly as I saw them fall.

Men of the Border Regiment rest during the battle of the Somme, 1916. They squat in 'funk holes' they have dug out of the side of the trench. Although the scene looks comfortable, most of the these men would have been badly bitten by lice. They tried to prevent them by running a lighted candle along the seams of their clothing, where the lice gathered. This was called 'chatting'. Rats and mice were also a problem.

The Treaty of Versailles, 1919

After the war, the victors met at the Palace of Versailles, near Paris, to tell Germany the terms of peace. Defeated Germany was not allowed to send any delegates, and had no choice but to accept whatever was decided. Most of the delegates wanted revenge. Only President Woodrow Wilson of the United States wanted a better world.

The main points of the Treaty of Versailles

1 Germany had to accept the blame for starting the war.

2 Germany had to pay £6,600 million, called **reparations**, for the damage done during the war.

3 Germany was forbidden to have submarines or an air force. She could have a navy of only six battleships, and an army of just 100,000 men. In addition, Germany was not allowed to place any troops in the Rhineland, the strip of land, 50 miles wide, next to France.

4 Germany lost land in Europe (*see map below*). Germany's colonies were given to Britain, France and Japan.

5 Land from the Austro-Hungarian empire was given to Italy, Poland, Rumania and Serbia (which became the country of Yugoslavia). The rest of the empire was split up into the nation-states of Czechoslovakia, Hungary and Austria.

6 The **League of Nations** was to be set up. About 40 countries joined. It tried to settle international problems peacefully, by discussion. It also tried to stop things like slavery and drugs.

The peace pleased nobody, and it made the Germans very angry. This anger helped to cause the Second World War.

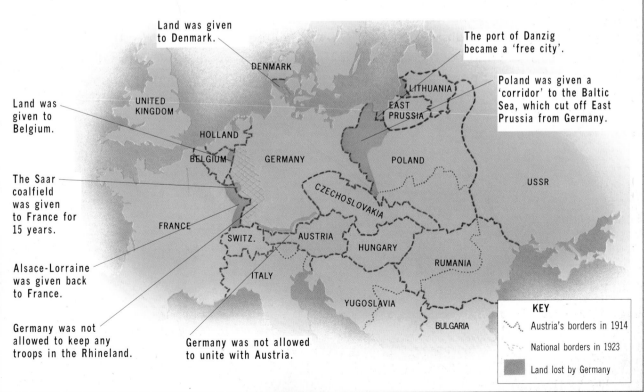

Land was given to Denmark.

The port of Danzig became a 'free city'.

Poland was given a 'corridor' to the Baltic Sea, which cut off East Prussia from Germany.

Land was given to Belgium.

The Saar coalfield was given to France for 15 years.

Alsace-Lorraine was given back to France.

Germany was not allowed to keep any troops in the Rhineland.

Germany was not allowed to unite with Austria.

DENMARK
LITHUANIA
UNITED KINGDOM
EAST PRUSSIA
HOLLAND
BELGIUM
GERMANY
POLAND
USSR
CZECHOSLOVAKIA
FRANCE
SWITZ.
AUSTRIA
HUNGARY
ITALY
RUMANIA
YUGOSLAVIA
BULGARIA

KEY
Austria's borders in 1914
National borders in 1923
Land lost by Germany

THE RUSSIAN REVOLUTION

Russia under the Tsars

Nicholas II became Tsar of Russia in 1894. Until 1905, he was an **autocrat**. He was totally in control of the government. If people rioted, he sent the Cossacks
5 (soldiers) to attack them. His secret police spies tracked down people who did not like the government and sent them to prison camps in Siberia.

In 1905, there was a revolution in Russia.
10 The Tsar was forced to accept a parliament. It was called the Duma. The Tsar still made all the decisions. If the members of the Duma disagreed with him, he sent them away.

Communism

15 Communists were people who agreed with the writer Karl Marx (1818–1883). Sometimes, they were called 'Marxists'. Marx had said that the Industrial Revolution had made the bourgeois (the
20 middle classes) rich and powerful. But they had made the workers their 'wage slaves'.

Nicholas blessing his troops. The Russian Army did badly in the First World War. In 1915, Tsar   35 Nicholas took control of the Russian Army. This was a disaster for Nicholas. People blamed him for the defeats. In March 1917, while Nicholas was away with the Army, there was a revolution in Russia.   40

Marx said it was time for the Proletariat (the workers) to rebel and take power for themselves. They would abolish private ownership, and hold all things in common. That is why they were called 'Communists'.   45
The most extreme Communists in Russia were a group called the **Bolsheviks**.

The map shows Russia in 1917. Russia stretched
25 4,000 miles from east to west. It was a very backward country. The Tsar ruled
30 over 150 million people. Most of them were poor peasants.

FINLAND
•Petrograd
GERMANY   •Moscow   SIBERIA

TURKEY

MONGOLIA

CHINA   Russian lands in 1917

The Death of Rasputin

Nicholas and Alexandra's son, Alexis, had the disease haemophilia. His blood would not clot, so he could not stop bleeding when he cut himself.

The only man who could stop the bleeding was a holy man called Rasputin. Fear can help the blood to clot, and some doctors think that Rasputin simply scared the poor boy to health! Some historians think he used hypnosis.

While Nicholas was away fighting with the Army, he left his wife Alexandra in charge of the government. Rasputin became her chief adviser. The Tsarina said that he was her only friend. Ministers who criticised him were sacked. Nicholas warned her, 'Our friend's opinions are very strange – you must be very careful'. But he did not stop her. People laughed at the Tsarina and hated Rasputin.

Rasputin came from a strange religious group called the Khlystis. Here he takes tea with a group of rich female followers. When they prayed together, the worshippers 'cried out, fell in convulsions and broke things'. Then they had wild orgies.

On the night of 29–30 December 1916 some Russian nobles decided to murder Rasputin. They invited him to a party. There, they offered him chocolate cakes and wine. Both were laced with cyanide. Rasputin liked chocolate, and he ate all the cakes and drank a glass of wine. But instead of shouting out and dying, Rasputin merely grew sleepy and asked for a cup of tea.

One of the nobles took out a gun and shot him. Rasputin did not die. Instead, he leapt to his feet, attacked them, and then ran out of the house.

Rasputin had always said that he was under the protection of God and could not be killed. The nobles began to fear that he was right. They chased him and shot him again. Then one of the nobles beat him viciously about the head.

The killers were scared, and starting to panic. They drove the body to the river. There, they dropped it into the freezing water. The current pulled it away downstream.

At last, the 'mad monk' was dead. He had drowned.

Causes of the March Revolution

In 1917 crowds of people rioted on the streets in Russia. The soldiers joined them. The members of the Duma joined the revolution. They forced the Tsar to abdicate (resign). What caused these amazing events? Here are ten ideas.

1 Workers' poverty?

This picture shows a metal worker's home in Petrograd, the capital city of Russia. Forty per cent of families had to share rooms. A report of 1902 described such rooms:

They are damp and unbelievably dirty . . . the plaster is crumbling, there are holes in the walls . . . legions of cockroaches and bugs . . . it is bitterly cold . . draughts in every corner.

2 Anger at the events of 1905?

On 22 January 1905, a crowd of poor people had gone on a march to beg the Tsar to help them. They thought he cared for them like a 'father'. But the Tsar ordered the Cossacks to shoot them. A thousand people died.
The day became known as 'Bloody Sunday'.

[The crowd goes away.]
A voice said nervously with a sob: 'Our fathers have shown us what they really are!' And somebody else said threateningly: 'We shall never forget this day.'
They walked quickly, in a close-packed crowd, many talking at once, and their voices merged with the dark, angry murmur.

Maxim Gorki (1868-1936), a Russian writer.

3 General unrest?

Most of the population is at present in a very troubled mood . . . .
People openly complain about the corrupt government, the unbelievable burdens of the war, the unbearable conditions of everyday life . . .
Everybody is saying that 'we are on the eve of great events.'

Police Reports for October 1916

4 Rasputin?

This political cartoon shows Rasputin holding the Tsar and Tsarina in his hands like puppets.

QUESTIONS

1 How does the artist show what he thinks of Rasputin?
2 How might a cartoon like this harm the government?

5 The Duma?

By 1917, Russia was clearly losing the war. The members of the Duma openly talked about the need to get rid of the Tsar.

A coup d'état is where a small group takes over the government.

General Krimov: The army will greet the news of a coup d'état with joy.
Deputy Shingarev: The general is right – a coup d'état is necessary, but who will dare lead it?
Deputy Shidlevsky: We cannot waste pity on the Tsar if he ruins Russia.

quoted in **T Downey**, *The USSR (1989)*

6 Young people who just wanted to stir up trouble?

There is a hooligan movement. Young people run and shout that there is no bread, simply to create excitement . . . If the weather was very cold they would all probably stay at home. But all this will pass and become calm.

Letter from the **Tsarina** *to Nicholas, 10 March 1917*

7 Hunger?

The winter of 1916–1917 was bitterly cold. The winter nights were 18 hours long. There were food shortages, fuel shortages and unemployment. On International Women's Day, 8 March 1917, thousands of people went on protest marches against the government.

The workers of the Vyborg district went on strike. They were angry because there was not enough black bread . . . At about 1 pm, crowds of workmen walked into the streets shouting 'Give us bread' . . .

Police Reports *for 8 March 1917*

8 Nicholas II?

On 12 March 1917, the soldiers in Petrograd disobeyed their officers and refused to fire on the crowds.

Rodzianko, the President of the Duma, telegraphed the Tsar:

The situation is growing worse. Something must be done immediately. Tomorrow is too late. The last hour has struck. The future of the country and the royal family is being decided.

The Tsar read the telegram and said:

Again, that fat-bellied Rodzianko has written me a lot of nonsense, which I won't even bother to answer.

On 13 March the government lost control of Petrograd. Members of the Duma met the Tsar and told him to abdicate.

10 Peasant poverty?

A peasant village. Peasants, however, took no part in the March revolution.

9 An act of cruelty?

Coco, the clown in Bertram Mills Circus, became famous in Britain in the 1950s. In 1917, he was living in Petrograd. These are his memories.

[The Cossacks had been ordered not to let anybody cross the bridge.] A tired old man, carrying a dinner-basin tied up in a red handkerchief, tried to push his way through the crowd. A Cossack stopped him. In a thin, piteous voice, the old man explained that if he could reach the other side of the river his daughter might let him have a little food. Looking sadly at him the Cossack refused and turned away. The old man trailed wearily after him . . .

This annoyed the Cossack officer . . With an angry oath the officer rode up to the old man and slashed him furiously across the face with his riding whip. The old fellow dropped his empty basin and began to cry.

Without a word, the Cossack drew his sabre [sword] and killed the officer.

Pandemonium broke loose. The Cossacks killed all their officers . . . A howling, impassioned mob streamed across the bridge and stormed the public buildings.

The revolution had begun.

From N Poliakoff, Coco the Clown

QUESTIONS

1 What class would the officer in Source 9 have come from?
2 What class would the soldier come from?

The Revolution after March 1917

Kerensky

15 March   **Dual Government**
Nicholas abdicated. The Duma set up a provisional (temporary) government. Alexander Kerensky became President.
At the same time, however, groups of workers set up the 'Soviets'. These were councils of people elected by the workers, peasants and soldiers. The workers obeyed the Soviets, which were as powerful as the government.

Lenin

16 April   **Lenin Returns**
Lenin was the leader of the Bolsheviks.
In 1906 he had gone into exile to escape the Tsar's secret police. In April 1917 the Germans smuggled him into Russia. He arrived at the Finland Station, in Petrograd.

16–20 July   **July Days**
There were riots in Petrograd.
The provisional government defeated the rioters.
Lenin was blamed.
He had to flee to Finland.

Kornilov

August   **The Kornilov Affair**
The Red Guards were the Bolshevik army.
Kornilov was a general in the Russian Army. He tried to overthrow the government.
The provisional government defeated him, but only with the help of the Red Guards. The Bolsheviks became very popular.

Trotsky

6–15 November   **The Ten Days**
On the night of 6 November, the Red Guards captured the important buildings in Petrograd. The revolution was organised by the Bolshevik leader, Leon Trotsky.
At 9.40 pm on 7 November, the Bolsheviks attacked the Winter Palace, the headquarters of the Provisional Government. They captured it.

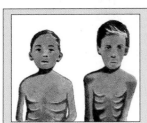

1918-1921   **The Civil War**
The 'White' armies tried to destroy the Revolution.
They were helped by armies from Britain, France and America.
The Bolsheviks fought back. The Tsar and his family were imprisoned, and then killed.
By 1922, the Bolsheviks were in charge of Russia.

INDIAN INDEPENDENCE

The Amritsar Incident

In 1919, India was part of the British
Empire. Many Indians wanted
independence. They formed the Indian
National Congress Party.

5 The British government passed two laws.
The Government of India Act of 1919 gave
the people of India some say in their local
government. But at the same time, the
Rowlatt laws gave British officials the right
10 to put people into prison without a trial.

Soon afterwards, there was a dreadful
incident. You can read the facts of the
case below.

April 1919

Mohandas Gandhi, the leader of the
15 Congress Party, organised a *hartal* (a day
of prayer).

Amritsar was a busy trading town in
northern India. It is the holy city of the
people who follow the Sikh religion and is
20 the site of their Golden Temple.

There was no trouble in Amritsar during
the *hartal* on 6 April 1919. On 10 April,
however, riots broke out. Four people were
killed, and Marcia Sherwood, a missionary,
25 was beaten up by a gang of youths and left
for dead.

Sunday, 13 April was a Sikh holy day.
Thousands of pilgrims came to the city.
General Reginald Dyer, the local British
30 military commander, gave an order
forbidding meetings of more than ten
people. That morning his men drove round
the city warning that any meetings would
be broken up by force.

35 That afternoon, a crowd gathered in a
local park called the Jallianwala Bagh.

There were between 5,000 and 20,000
people (estimates vary). Some listened to
speeches criticising the Rowlatt laws.

Late in the afternoon, Dyer arrived with 40
a troop of soldiers. Without warning, they
fired 1,650 rounds into the packed crowd.
Then they left. Officially, 379 people were
killed, but many more people lost their
lives. They crawled back, wounded, to 4
die in their own homes.

After Amritsar

Dyer was forced to resign, *but*:
- the House of Lords voted that Dyer had
  acted correctly.
- *The Morning Post* newspaper raised 5
  £26,000 for Dyer – 'The Man who
  saved India'.

On 19 April, Dyer visited Marcia Sherwood in
hospital. 'A helpless woman has been mercilessly
beaten in a most cruel manner by a lot of cowards,'
he said. A whipping frame was put up in the street
where she was attacked. Six Indian youths – who
had nothing to do with the crime – were whipped.
Dyer ordered that any Indian who needed to go
down the street had to crawl along it.

The **Amritsar massacre** was one of the greatest disgraces in the history of the British Empire.

The British government set up the Hunter Commission to investigate the incident. It officially rejected Dyer's excuse – that he was trying to stop a rebellion. It concluded:

General Dyer acted beyond . . . what any reasonable man could have thought to be necessary.

Few British history books, however, openly condemn Dyer's action. This page records the comments of three historians about 'the Amritsar massacre'.

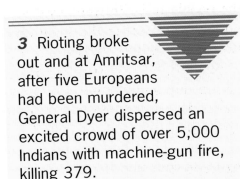

1 There were many Indians who said that [the Government of India Act] did not go far enough . . .
[There was] an outburst of strikes and violence in its very first year. The worst incident occurred at Amritsar: a British general, determined to protect European lives and property, ordered his troops to fire on a large crowd which had defied his instructions to disperse.

M N Duffy, *The 20th Century (1965)*

2 In an atmosphere of disorder and rebellion came the episode at Amritsar, in April 1919, when General Dyer opened fire on an unarmed crowd who, after the murder of four Europeans, refused an order to disperse.

L C B Seaman, *Post-Victorian Britain (1966)*

3 Rioting broke out and at Amritsar, after five Europeans had been murdered, General Dyer dispersed an excited crowd of over 5,000 Indians with machine-gun fire, killing 379.

N Lowe, *Mastering World History (1982)*
General Dyer estimated the size of the crowd at 5,000.

QUESTIONS

1 Can you find any differences between the facts in sources 1–3, and the facts given in the account on page 32?
2 Explain how source 2 describes the events in such a way as to give completely the wrong impression.
3 Suggest reasons why all these textbooks try to 'explain away' the Amritsar massacre.

India's Independence

The Amritsar incident convinced Gandhi that the British had to leave India. 'When a government takes up arms against its unarmed subjects, then it has lost the right
5 to govern,' he wrote. The Congress Party continued to demand independence.

Gandhi was both a clever politician and a holy man. He developed the idea of non-violent protest. He encouraged people
10 to disobey unfair laws. As a result, in the 28 years between 1919 and 1947, Gandhi spent 2,388 days in prison.

Gandhi's Salt March of 1930 (*see picture below*) is an example of non-violent protest.
15 Before 1930, Indians were not allowed to make their own salt, or collect it from the sea-shore. They had to buy it. There was a tax on salt, and the money went to the British government. Salt was a necessity of
20 life, and the law especially harmed the poorest people.

Gandhi asked the British government in India, to abolish the salt rules. When they did not do as he asked, on 12 March, 1930, he and 78 followers set off on a
25 200-mile march to the sea. 'I want world sympathy in this battle of right against might', he wrote.

By the time he arrived, the crowd was tens of thousands strong. There, Gandhi
30 simply scraped a pinch of salt from the surface of the sand.

All over India, people disobeyed the law and made their own salt. After arresting 100,000 people, the British government
35 gave way and abolished the salt laws.

Not all Gandhi's supporters believed in non-violent protest. His campaigns were usually followed by rioting and murders all over India. The 1935 Government of India
40 Act gave Indians control of everything except defence and foreign affairs. The Congress Party, however, continued to demand complete independence from Britain.
45

The Road to Independence

During the Second World War, some Indians refused to help the
British fight the Japanese. The Indian politician S C Bose even
moved to Tokyo, and tried to raise an Army of Liberation to drive
the British from India. In 1942, there were anti-British riots in
50 northern India.

In August 1947 the British left India. British India was divided
into the three countries of India, Pakistan and Burma.

Two-thirds of Indians were Hindus. The Muslims –
led by Muhammad Ali Jinnah – demanded a separate state
55 for Muslims, called Pakistan. Tensions grew between
Hindus and Muslims, and they began to attack
each other. Hundreds of thousands of people died.

In September 1947, Gandhi began a four-day
fast to try to stop the violence. His fast, and the
60 coming of independence, helped to calm the
violence

Mahatma Gandhi

Gandhi has been described as a saint.
Albert Einstein said of him:

Generations will follow and will
65 hardly believe that such a man of flesh
and blood has ever walked the earth.

He prayed every day. He said it was wrong to
kill any living thing; he was a vegetarian who
lived mainly on peanut butter and lemons. He said it was
70 wrong to feast when others were hungry. He wore only the
cheapest glasses, and refused false teeth. He visited the king
dressed only in the loincloth he had made himself. When asked if
he thought he had enough on, Gandhi joked, 'The King is wearing
enough for both of us.'
75 Unlike many Indians, Gandhi accepted women as equals, and
allowed the lowest caste of people (the 'Untouchables') to come into
his house. He called them *Harijans* (children of God). He once
cleaned out toilets to show that all work is honourable. The Indians
respected Gandhi so much that they gave him the title, Mahatma,
80 meaning 'Great Soul'.

Gandhi was shot dead in 1948, by a Hindu Indian who
thought Gandhi was damaging the Hindu faith.

35

BRITAIN IN THE 1920S

'A Land Fit for Heroes'

After 1918, the soldiers came back from the war. Lloyd George, the British Prime Minister, said they deserved 'a land fit for heroes to live in'. In the same year, for the
5 first time in British history, women over 30 were allowed to vote.

There was a boom in industry. People rushed out to buy the things they hadn't been able to buy during the war. Factory
10 workers worked overtime. They were paid more money. This meant that they could buy even more.

Soon, however, the boom ended. Unemployment grew. There was trouble in
15 the coal industry in 1921, when the mine-owners cut wages. The miners went on strike. After a month, they were defeated.

??? QUESTION ???

Find two reasons on this page why the Labour government of 1924 fell from power.

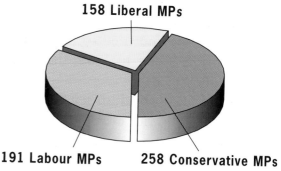

158 Liberal MPs

191 Labour MPs   258 Conservative MPs

The Labour government of 1924 was a 'minority' government. It did not have a majority of MPs in the House of Commons. It ruled only with the 20 support of the Liberal Party. When the Liberals voted against Labour, the government was forced to resign.

The First Labour Government.

In January 1924, a Labour government took power in Britain for the first time. 25 Ramsay MacDonald became Prime Minister. The new government helped local councils build council houses. It increased old age pensions and dole money. It said that all children must be given secondary 30 education.

The government, however, was a minority government (*see picture, above*) and after nine months it fell from power.

Left to right. Ramsay MacDonald 35 with his Labour ministers: J H Thomas, Arthur Henderson and J R Clynes. Clynes remembered how strange it felt when 'MacDonald the clerk , Thomas the engine-driver, 40 Henderson the labourer and Clynes the mill-hand' went to meet George V. Some workers distrusted the Labour government. One shipyard worker did not like the new Labour 45 ministers wearing smart suits and top hats. 'It's a lum [tall] hat government like all the rest' he shouted.

Stanley Baldwin, the Prime Minister taking part in a BBC news broadcast.

The General Strike

Trouble in the coal industry continued. In 1925, the mine-owners proposed another cut in the miners' wages. They also wanted to increase the hours the miners worked. The miners' leader, Herbert Smith, gave the miners' reply: 'Nowt doin', he said.

This time, however, the miners were supported by workers in the transport, printing, iron and steel, chemicals, electricity and gas industries. If it came to a strike, it would be a General Strike.

The miners took up the slogan, 'Not a minute on the day; not a penny off the pay.' The mine-owners continued to demand a cut in wages and an increase in the hours of work. On Monday, 3 May 1926, the Trades Union Congress (TUC) called a General Strike.

The Strike lasted nine days. At first it was successful. As time went on, however, volunteer workers began to undermine the strike action. Also, the government took strong measures to destroy the strike. Some strikers replied with violence. On 12 May 1926, the leaders of the TUC called off the Strike. Their money for strike pay was running out, and they feared the Strike would end up in a violent revolution.

The miners fought on alone until 30 November, when they were forced to return to work – for less money and longer hours. They had lost everything.

In 1927, the Trades Disputes Act made general strikes illegal. The strike of 1926 was the first General Strike in Britain, and it was the last.

A soup kitchen set up for hungry miners.

The Nine Days

1 Goods held up because of the strike at Paddington station in London. There were complete stoppages on the railways, at the docks, and in the printing and iron industries. Strikebreakers kept the electricity stations working.

2 In this photo, people are going to work on a steam lorry. For many people, the strike was just a bit of fun. Children enjoyed getting free lifts from volunteer drivers. For some, the strike was an extra holiday.

3 Some people volunteered to keep the railways running. Most volunteers were middle class. On 10 May three people were killed when a volunteer train driver ran into a goods train.

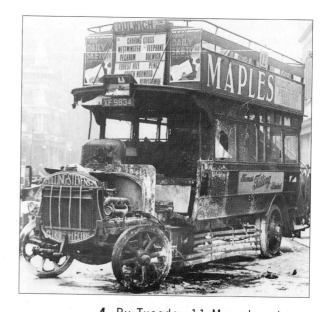

4 By Tuesday 11 May almost a thousand buses were on the road, driven by volunteer bus drivers. The volunteers had many accidents. Strikers threw stones at buses, and sometimes set them on fire.

5 On Monday 10 May strikers derailed *The Flying Scotsman* near Newcastle.

7 The government appointed 226,000 Special constables. It sent the army to possible trouble spots such as the coal mining areas. Communists and trade union leaders were arrested.

6 On Saturday 8 May armoured cars escorted a convoy of food lorries away from the docks in London. Look at the number of policemen in the photograph. Did the government really need to use them?

9 There were riots in a number of places – especially in the East End of London, where many people were Communists.

8 On Monday 10 May police and strikers in Plymouth played against each other in a football match. The strikers won, 2–1.

10 The TUC published The *British Worker*. It was difficult to print the newspaper because the government took away the paper.

The government published The *British Gazette*. It also controlled what the BBC could say. In the war of words, the government won.

11 J H Thomas was on the TUC General Council. But he did not want a General Strike. He had secret talks with the mine-owners and the government. On 11 May he persuaded the TUC to call off the strike.

Living through the Strike

People are different. They come from different backgrounds and have different views. The General Strike affected them in different ways.

Here are two people's reactions to the strike.

1 When I arrived at Paddington there were no ordinary porters, but I met a very good-looking man, medical student he looked like, who seized my suitcases. I wanted to get to Baker Street, so he and I explored passages with locked gates; he knew nothing about it, apparently . . .

It is perfectly splendid to hear, instead of 'Arrer 'n 'Uxbridge', a beautiful Oxford voice crying, 'Harrow and Uxbridge train'. Ticket collectors say, 'Thank you very much'.

One man in plus fours waved a green flag. Nothing happened. He waved again, and blew a whistle, then said to the driver in hurt tones, 'I say, you might *go.*' It's all very jolly and such an improvement on the ordinary humdrum state of things.

2 This is a transcript of a radio interview, made in the 1970s.

'Blacklegs' were strike-breakers, men who did the jobs of the people who were on strike.

1926 was the best year for weather that I can remember. We had a lovely summer. People always said that God had been good to the pitman. Because they needed the sun. And although we had no money – we hadn't any money at all – we still kind of *managed.*

During the strike – we did – in this part of the world one of the recreations was watching the blacklegs being marched up from the pit with a whole troop of policemen . . .

The men didn't – you weren't allowed to – shout at them or anything. You just stood and watched. Sometimes the blacklegs shouted back but the people just stood silent and watched them go by.

For food, well naturally we lived pretty mean. Very hard on the wives, trying to make ends meet – without any! [He laughs.] It was funny. What we got instead of meat was broth . . It's not bad, quite reasonable.

? ? ? QUESTION ? ? ?

Read the sources and work out what kind of person each speaker was. How does this explain their different attitudes to the strike?

The Changing Rôle of Women

These five illustrations show British women's lives at different times during the twentieth century.

4 An advertisement for a kitchen cleaner.

1 Women laying the road.

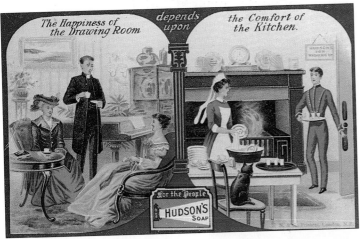

2 Ladies and maids in a wealthy household.

3 Ruby Loftus making a breech-ring.

5 Music and dancing.

MUSSOLINI'S ITALY

Italy in 1919

The Italians were angry about six things.

1 The First World War
600,000 Italians had died, but all Italy got out of the war was a little land.

2 Parliament
There were many parties in Parliament. No party could get a majority. Governments were too weak to pass the laws that were needed.

3 The Communists
Rich Italians were afraid that the Communists would take over. Italian business-men also hated the trade unions, which organised strikes for higher wages.

4 Poverty
In 1915–1919, prices rose 500 per cent. A tenth of the workforce was unemployed. Many Italians were very poor, especially in southern Italy.

5 Lawlessness
Bands of ex-soldiers roamed the country stealing and murdering.

6 The Problem of the Church
The Pope – the head of the Roman Catholic Church – hated the Italian government. When Italy became a united country in 1870, it had taken land once ruled by the popes. Many Italians were Catholics and agreed with the Pope.

Mussolini as a soldier. Like Adolf Hitler, Mussolini rose to the rank of corporal.

The Italians did what everybody does – THEY BLAMED THE GOVERNMENT for all these problems.

Italian Fascism

Benito Mussolini was the founder of Fascism. He had once been a teacher! He formed his Fascist Party in 1919. Many ex-soldiers supported him. He gave them a black uniform. They were called 'blackshirts'. In 1922, Mussolini announced that his Fascists were going to march on Rome to take over the government. All over Italy, Fascist gangs took over town halls and police stations. The King of Italy gave in. In October 1922 he asked Mussolini to become Prime Minister.

By 1925 Mussolini had total power. The Fascists' wanted:

The *fasces* – symbol of Italian Fascism. In the time of the Roman Empire it was carried in front of judges. The bundle of wooden sticks symbolised strength, unity and law.

A A strong economy
Mussolini encouraged farming and industry. Poor people were given welfare payments. The government built roads and railways, which helped industry and gave employment to people.

B Law and order
The Fascist Party controlled the newspapers and radio. Teachers had to wear a uniform and teach Fascist ideas.

C A strong government
Mussolini became *Il Duce* ('the leader'). He made all the laws. Opposition parties were forbidden. Mussolini's blackshirts beat up or murdered his opponents.

D Weak Trade Unions
In 1926, Mussolini abolished trade unions. Strikes were forbidden.

E Agreement with the Church
In 1929, Mussolini made an agreement with the Pope. Roman Catholicism became the official religion of Italy. The Pope supported Mussolini.

F A strong Foreign Policy
In 1935-6 Mussolini conquered Ethiopia. In 1937 he made an alliance with Germany and Japan. In 1940 he entered the Second World War on Germany's side.

Mussolini became a totalitarian dictator. **Totalitarian** means the State has power over every aspect of a person's life. A **dictator** is one person who makes all the decisions of government.

HITLER'S GERMANY

Adolf Hitler was born in 1889. He did not come from an important family. He was not even born in Germany. He was the son of an Austrian customs official. His father
5 was a hard-drinking bully, who beat his son. He died when Hitler was 14. Hitler's mother spoiled him. She died when he was 18.

One of Hitler's teachers remembered what
10 he had been like at school:

He wanted his own way. He was boastful, bad-tempered [and] lazy . . . He ignored advice and got angry if he was told off. At the same time, he demanded unquestioning
15 obedience from his fellow pupils.

Hitler despised all his teachers except his History teacher, who taught him to love Germany.

In 1907 Hitler ran away to Vienna. He wanted to be an artist but he failed to get 20 into art college. He became a dropout. He hung round the night shelters. He learned to hate. Most of all, he hated the Jews and the Communists. The Jews, he decided, were inferior. Communism would ruin 25 Germany, he said.

In 1914, Hitler joined the German Army. He was blinded in a gas attack. He won the Iron Cross medal twice.

But in 1918, after Germany's defeat, he 30 returned to the night shelters. He was bitter and angry. He said that the German Army had lost because it had been betrayed. He was sure it had been betrayed by . . . the Jews and the Communists. 35

In Vienna

He was 21 when I knew him. He wore an ancient black overcoat, which had been given to him by an old clothes dealer, a Hungarian Jew, and which reached down over his knees. From under a greasy bowler hat, his hair hung down over his coat collar. His thin and hungry face was covered with a black beard, above which his large, staring eyes were the one prominent feature. He was lazy and moody. He disliked regular work. He neither smoked nor drank, and he was too shy and awkward to have any success with women. His passions were reading newspapers and talking politics. He would hang around the night-shelters, living on the bread and soup that he got there, discussing politics. He often got involved in heated arguments. When he got excited he would shout and wave his arms. Sometimes people laughed at him; at other times they were oddly impressed.

One evening, I remember, Hitler went to a cinema where the film *The Tunnel* was being shown. In this film a rebel appears who rouses the working masses to rebellion by his speeches. Hitler almost went crazy. The impression it made on him was so strong that for days he talked of nothing but the power of the spoken word.

*The memories of **Reinhold Hanisch**, a tramp who lived in the same hostel as Hitler.*

Hitler's father, Alois, was illegitimate. At first Alois took his mother's surname of Schicklgruber, but later changed his surname to Hitler. Adolf was always grateful to his father for this. Hitler, he said, 'was nice, and easy to remember'.

Would Hitler have come to power if he had been called Schicklgruber? Would the crowds have shouted 'Heil Schicklgruber'?

Hitler could draw buildings well. But this drawing of his teacher shows why he failed to get into art college.

QUESTION

Suggest reasons why *The Tunnel* had such an effect on Hitler at this time in his life.

45

How Hitler Rose to Power

28 June 1919
The Treaty of Versailles

The Germans had to pay 'reparations' for the First World War. They were angry.

14 September 1919
Hitler joined the Nazis

Hitler joined the Nazi Party. He was a brilliant speaker. In 1920 he became its leader.

1921
The SA was formed

Hitler formed a group of soldiers and thugs – the SA – to attack rival parties.

1927
Hitler Youth

Hitler formed the Hitler Youth. In their spare time, young people did sports. They also studied Nazi ideas, and were taught to obey Hitler.

1928
Nazi Propaganda

Josef Goebbels was put in charge of Nazi propaganda. The Nazis used radio, newspaper and mass rallies to get their ideas across.

1929-1932
World Depression

There was bad unemployment. A quarter of the German workforce was out of work. Some people starved to death. Support for the Nazis grew.

23 March 1933
The Enabling Act

The Reichstag (the German parliament) gave Hitler the power to make his own laws.

26 April 1933
The Gestapo

Nazis were put in charge of the local government and police. The Nazis formed the Gestapo (the secret police)

2 May 1933
Trade Unions were abolished

ToD DER LÜGE

Marxismus

The Trade Unions' offices were closed down, their money was confiscated, and their leaders were put in prison.

1923
'Hyperinflation'

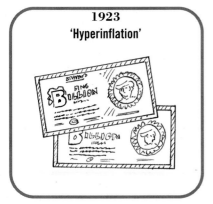

Prices rose rapidly ('hyperinflation'). People
were ruined. The Nazi party grew quickly.

8–9 November 1923
Beer Hall Putsch

Hitler led a 'putsch' (a revolution) in
Munich. It failed. Sixteen Nazis were killed.
Hitler was put in prison.

1924
Mein Kampf

In prison, Hitler wrote *Mein Kampf* (meaning
'My Struggle'). He explained his ideas.
He became popular.

30 January 1933
Hitler became Chancellor

President Hindenburg made Hitler
Chancellor. He thought he could control
Hitler.

27 February 1933
The Reichstag Fire

The Reichstag (the German parliament)
burned down. Hitler used the fire as an
excuse to arrest his Communist opponents.

5 March 1933
General election

In the election, 44% of the people voted
Nazi. This did not give Hitler a majority, so
he put the 81 Communist deputies in prison.

14 July 1933
Opposition Parties banned

The Nazi Party was declared 'the only
political party in Germany'.

30 June 1934
The Night of the Long Knives

Hitler used his personal body-guards
(the SS) to kill hundreds of SA men.

19 August 1934
Hitler became Führer

President Hindenburg died on 2 August.
Hitler declared himself Führer – President,
Chancellor, and Commander of the Army.

Hitler the Demagogue

A 'demagogue' is a leader who can 'rouse the masses'.
Hitler had the power to arouse mass support. How?

1 Order and hope

My mother saw an SA parade . . . .
  The sight of discipline in a time of chaos, the
sense of energy in an atmosphere of universal
hopelessness, seems to have won her over. At any rate,
without having heard a speech or read a pamphlet, she
joined the [Nazi] party.

from **Albert Speer**, Inside the Third Reich *(1970).*
Speer was Hitler's chief architect and his
Minister for Armaments.

2 Hypnotic excitement

Suddenly there was a movement at the back entrance. Words of command. The speaker on the platform stopped in mid-sentence. Everybody jumped up, saluting. And right through the shouting crowds and streaming flags came the one they were waiting for . . . He passed by me quite close . . . I saw his thin, pale features twisted as if by inward rage, cold flames darting from his staring eyes, which seemed to be searching out enemies to be defeated.

Did the crowd give him this mysterious power? Did it come from him to them?

Professor K A von Muller, *a German History professor, remembering a Nazi rally in 1923.*

3 Emotions and patriotism

He was holding the masses, and me with them, under an hypnotic spell by the sheer force of his beliefs . . . I do not know how to describe the emotions that swept over me as I heard this man. His words were like a whip. When he spoke of the disgrace of Germany, I felt ready to spring on any enemy . . .

Of course I was ripe for this experience. I was a man of thirty-two, weary with disgust and disillusionment, a wanderer seeking a cause, a patriot seeking an outlet for his patriotism.

Karl Ludecke, *an early follower of Hitler, remembering the first time he heard Hitler speak (in 1924).*

4 Religion and militarism

This morning's opening meeting . . . was more than just a gorgeous show; it also had something of the mystery and religious fervour of an Easter Mass in a great Cathedral . . .

A highly-trained group of fanatical Nazi youths broke into a perfect goose-step . . . I felt for the first time this morning how it touches the strange soul of the German people. They jumped up and shouted: 'We want one Leader! Nothing for us! Everything for Germany! Heil Hitler!'

William Shirer, Berlin Diary, *6 September 1934. Shirer was an American news reporter. The goose-step was the slow, high-kicking Nazi way of marching.*

Why did Germans Vote for the Nazis?

All these posters appeared in Germany in the 1920s and 1930s. They were designed to appeal to different sections of the German people, to persuade them to vote Nazi.

translation:
Work and Bread
vote list 1

translation:
We Farmers are cleaning out the dung
Vote list 2, National Socialist.

◁ Vote for the Nazi candidates to get jobs and food. In 1932, six million people were out of work in Germany.

△ A farmer shovels out Communist rebels and Jewish money-men. Many farmers owed money to Jewish businessmen and bankers.

translation:
Faith. Order.

translation:
VICTORY or BOLSHEVISM

◁ Bolshevism is Communism. Many Germans feared that if the Communists took over, there would be a 'Terror' in Germany, as there was in Stalin's Russia.

△ Germany (Deutschland) clings onto Hitler, whose flag reads '**Faith. Order.**' Many Germans worried about the violence on the streets between the Communists and Nazis.

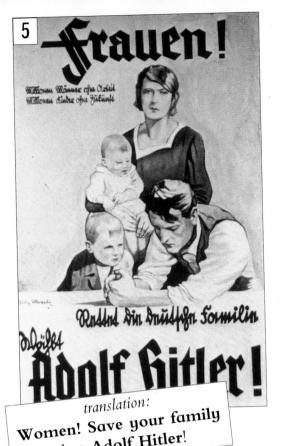

translation:
**Women! Save your family
elect Adolf Hitler!**

△ Mothers were affected by the
depression more badly than other people,
for they had to watch their families starving.

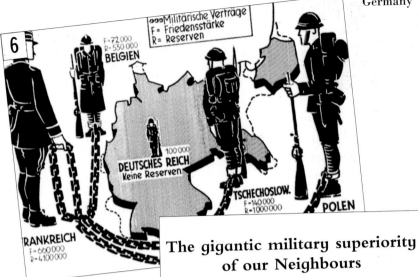

**The gigantic military superiority
of our Neighbours**

△ The map shows the effects of the Versailles Treaty.
The poster says that Germany has a peacetime army
of only 100,000 and no reserves. Meanwhile, the huge
armies of their neighbours are linked to France by the
chains of Military Treaties.

??? QUESTIONS ???

For each poster, ask yourself:
- Who was it trying to appeal to?
- How was it trying to appeal to them?
- How successful do you think it would
  have been?

◁ Hitler had been a lance
corporal in the First World
War. Hindenburg – who was
supreme commander of the
German Army during the
First World War – became
President of Germany in
1925.

translation:
**The FIELD MARSHAL and
the LANCE CORPORAL**
Fight with us for peace and
Equal Rights.

▷ Hitler had fought
with the German
Army on the
Western Front in
the First World
War.

**WORKER
Choose the
Front-soldier**

51

The Nazi Terror

Hitler believed in the use of force. 'Our motto shall be – if you are not a true German, I will bash your skull in', he declared. Children were encouraged to report their parents to their teachers if they spoke against the Führer. Every set of flats had a 'staircase ruler' who reported grumblers to the police.

Many of the Nazis' opponents were killed or sent to the concentration camps.

The source below tells the story of a man named Leidler, who had been a member of the moderate socialist Social Democratic Party. The date is some time after July 1933.

The *Reichsbanner* (the military wing of the Social Democratic Party) wanted to throw Hitler out of power by means of a revolution. The Gestapo was the German secret police. The SS was a Nazi terror organisation.

An unknown man knocked at Leidler's door and asked for him by name. Leidler took him in. It was raining and the man was wet. The man showed Leidler a *Reichsbanner* membership book and told him that he was on the run from the Gestapo. He told Leidler that the *Reichsbanner* had rebelled and was fighting the Nazis. Did Leidler have any weapons? Could he supply the names of any loyal *Reichsbanner* men in the area?

Leidler answered 'no' to each question and added, 'I'm through. I've had the shit kicked out of me. All I can do is put you up overnight and feed you, which I'd do for any human being on a night like this.'

In the morning, after breakfast, the man went to the door and, just before he left, turned his lapel back and showed Leidler an SS button. Then he left wordlessly.

quoted in **T Howarth**, Twentieth Century History (1979)

Chapter 7

The Hitler Youth

The Nazis made great efforts to attract young people into their ranks. The girls and boys were indoctrinated (brainwashed) to think like Nazis. These sources suggest reasons why young people joined the Nazi youth movement, the Hitler Youth.

Unity of youth in the Hitler Youth. This poster shows Jews and Communists running in terror from a drummer of the Hitler Youth.

1 We heard a great deal of talk about Fatherland, comradeship, and love of homeland . . .

But one more thing that attracted us with a mysterious force and pulled us along – namely, the compact columns of marching youths with waving flags, eyes looking straight ahead, and the beat of drums and singing . . .

In the evenings we met at the den, and someone would read, or we sang, or played games and did craft work. We heard that we should live for a great cause. We were taken seriously.

Inge Scholl, Die Weisse Rose *1961*

2 One day the head of the firm drew me aside. 'Adolf', he said, 'do me a favour and join the Hitler Youth, It'll be better for you and better for the firm. You know, of course, that every firm has its SA man. We haven't one. Moreover, we're Jewish. Please join the Hitler Youth. Then at least we shall have a Nazi on the premises.'

from **Hans Siemen**, Hitler Youth *1940*

3 In the class which is taught by teacher A there are ten members of the [local Catholic] Youth Club . . . Teacher A exerts such pressure on the members of the Youth Club that it is almost unbearable for the boys. For example:. . . a member of the Hitler Youth had come back to the Catholic Youth Club. When Mr A heard of this he threatened he would set him forty sums every time he stayed away from the Hitler Youth parade. This was made even worse by his threat of a beating as well . .

Letter of complaint from a **Catholic priest** *to the district leader of the Nazi Party.*

? ? ? **QUESTION** ? ? ?

What different things attracted these young people of to the Hitler Youth?

53

Life in Nazi Germany

The ideas, values and attitudes of people in Nazi Germany were very different to today, as is shown in these sources.

1 Boy scouts?

When an instructor blows a whistle, we have to start building dug-outs. There are about a dozen of us, each with a spade. And we all start to dig like lunatics.

Because in front of us are ten Benz armoured cars waiting, their engines slowly ticking over.

We have twenty minutes to dig the hole which will shelter us. Which will save our lives. It's every man for himself. We aren't comrades any more . . .

Never mind, I must dig and dig and dig.

I can hear an engine revving up. It is a sinister and menacing sound.

This is it. They're moving off, advancing, straight ahead. The drivers have been ordered to take no notice of anybody clumsy or foolish enough to get in the way. They thunder towards our dug-outs.

With wild shouts the boys jump into the holes they have dug, burrowing into the earth, burying their faces against the damp clay.

In front of me, like some monster in a nightmare, the Benz lumbers forward, its engine roaring. It's getting bigger and bigger, and bigger still . . .

They're past.

Of course, some of our chaps are killed. But none are cowards.

Thus do we learn courage – at the risk of our lives.

P Neumann, *Other Men's Graves (1958)*

Boys at a Nazi Training School.

2 Following orders

SS Major-General Ohlendorf confessed to the murder of 90,000 Jews in Russia. He was asked by his Defence lawyer whether he had ever felt doubts about the tasks he was required to carry out. He answered, 'Yes, of course.'

'And how was it,' the Defence lawyer continued, 'that they were carried out despite these doubts?'

Ohlendorf replied: 'Because to me it is unthinkable that a subordinate should not carry out orders given by the leaders of the state.'

E Crankshaw, *Gestapo (1966)*

3 Guide Camp?

'Tell me, Fraulein Liselotte, if I may call you Liselotte, you seem so charming, and kind. What happens here? I mean, in general. Naturally, I'm not just talking about the genetic part of it, but . . .'

'But you're dying to know how we all go to bed together according to Nazi rules?' she broke in, smiling again.

I was rather embarrassed. I must have blushed.

'That isn't quite what I meant. I want to know the routine here.'

She became more serious.

'All I can tell you is that we live in dormitories of six or twelve beds. The girls who are . . . chosen, are moved to another section, which deals with the legal details of the partnership, and of course any births which result from it. Because we must remember that that's what we're all here for,' she ended quietly, looking away.

'A strange thing for your country to ask you to do, don't you agree?'

P Neumann, *Other Men's Graves (1958)*

4 A true Aryan

Himmler's ideal man was a fair-haired, blue-eyed superhuman athlete whose values came from the knight-farmers of the Middle Ages.
He was a man who despised most developments in modern culture, though he might play accepted music on the violin or read accepted books.
Though he might well be in private a kindly husband and a generous father, he was essentially a destructive man, ready to act on the vilest or most stupid orders.

B Manvell *and* **H Fraenkel**, *Himmler (1965)*

5 The SS

After 1932, every member of the SS had to carry his Family Book and get a Certificate of Approval for any girl he wanted to marry. The SS kept 'stud books' for every SS man, whose Aryan blood had to be proved uncontaminated [by Jewish blood] as far back as 1750.

6 'Protective custody'

The argument behind [the concentration camps] was brutally simple: certain types of people refused to behave like everyone else – so why not lock them up? The anti-social elements included beggars, gypsies, prostitutes, 'grumblers', alcoholics, hooligans and what the Nazis called 'mental cases'. Homosexuals were definitely 'anti-social', and so were people who refused to work.

By the summer of 1939 there were about 25,000 prisoners in the camps.

T Howarth, *Twentieth Century History (1979)*

STALIN'S RUSSIA

In 1923, Russia became the Union of Soviet Socialist Republics (USSR). It was often called the Soviet Union.

5 When Lenin died in January 1924, Josef Stalin came to power. Until his death in 1953, Stalin was unquestioned dictator of the USSR.

Stalin believed that Russia was surrounded by enemies who wanted to destroy her. He
10 realised that Russia had to be modernised and united. In 1931, he warned the Russian people:

We are 50 to 100 years behind the advanced countries. We must catch up this
15 distance in ten years. Either we do it, or they crush us.

Stalin was right. In 1941, Hitler invaded the USSR. But Stalin had made the Soviet Union ready. Hitler was defeated.

This Russian poster of the 1930s proclaims: 'Seven 20 Problems – One Answer'. It advertises the Five Year Plan (see page 57). The Plan, it says, will be 'completed in 4 years!'
In the poster, can you spot among Russia's enemies:
• Mussolini, 25
• a German Nazi,
• Stalin's enemy Trotsky (a rival Communist. Stalin claimed he was paid by Hitler),
• the Pope,
• a Japanese soldier? 30

1 A poem printed in *Pravda* (1935)

O great Stalin, O leader of the
  peoples,
You brought man to birth.
You make the crops grow,
You bring back the good times,
You cause the spring to bloom,
  and music to play.
You, glory of my spring,
The sun which shines into millions
  of hearts.

Pravda *was the official newspaper of the Communist Party.*

2 A Soviet joke from the 1930s

Stalin wanted to know what people really thought about him, so he went in disguise to a cinema.

A newsreel was shown which naturally highlighted Stalin in every scene. All the audience stood up amidst thunderous, never-ending applause. Stalin stayed modestly in his seat.

After a few moments the man next to Stalin nudged him and said: 'Most people feel the same as you, comrade. But it would be safer if you stood up.'

Stalin's plan to modernise and unite Russia had three points.

1 'Collectivisation' to increase food production

Stalin abolished the small peasant farms. He united them into large 'collective' farms. The whole village farmed the collective, using modern technology such as tractors. When the rich peasants, the **kulaks**, tried to resist Stalin's changes, about seven million kulaks were sent to workcamps.

2 'Five Year Plans' (1928–33 and 1933–37)

The Five Year Plans were drives to produce more oil, coal, steel and electricity. New industrial towns were built in the east of the USSR. Many of the workers there were kulaks or other opponents of Stalin. Some, however, were enthusiastic young communists called 'Pioneers'.

3 The Terror (1934–1938)

Russia, said Stalin, also had to be united. He demanded complete support for his policies. The NKVD (the secret police) sent thousands of people to a system of workcamps called the **gulag**. Many others were taken away and shot. Important Communists were put on trial at public **show trials**. They were made to look foolish, and forced to confess to crimes they did not do.

During the Terror, Stalin's opponents simply disappeared. It was as though they had never existed. Teachers were sent new pages to paste over the pages of textbooks which mentioned people who had been fallen out of Stalin's favour.

? ? ? **QUESTION** ? ? ?

Read Sources 1 and 2 on page 56. Did the writer of Source 1 really like Stalin?

This photograph of Stalin and his colleagues, taken in 1925, has been re-touched for the 1949 version shown beneath it. How many people are missing?

AMERICA BETWEEN THE WARS

Prohibition

On St Valentine's Day, 1929, seven men sat talking in the SMC Cartage Company garage in North Clark Street, Chicago. Five of them were gangsters. They were
5 members of George 'Bugs' Moran's gangland outfit. With them were Reinhardt Schwimmer, a wealthy optician who liked to be seen with gangsters, and John May, the garage mechanic. Two men, dressed as
10 policemen, went into the garage. They lined the seven men up against the wall and took their guns.

Suddenly, two hit-men – 'torpedoes', as they were called – burst into the garage.
15 One carried a sawn-off shotgun, the other had a machine gun. They blazed away at the helpless men. Twenty seconds later, it was all over. One man's head had been blown open. Another man was slumped
20 over a chair; shreds of skin dangled between his splintered bones and shattered teeth. Four corpses, riddled with machine gun bullets, stared lifelessly at the ceiling. 'My God!' gasped Sergeant Fred O'Neill,
25 the first real policeman to arrive on the scene. 'What a massacre!'

In 1929, the most powerful Chicago gang leader was Al Capone. Since 1920 it had been against the law in America to sell
30 alcohol. This was known as 'Prohibition'. Gangsters like Capone made a fortune from 'bootlegging' – making and smuggling booze for the 'speakeasies' (the illegal bars where you could still get
35 a drink). Capone's speakeasies were places of luxury, with a bar and dance hall, gambling tables at the back and rooms upstairs for prostitutes.

Capone was king of Chicago. He bribed Chicago's politicians and judges. Corrupt
40 policemen guarded his gambling joints. He controlled most of the other gangsters in Chicago. Moran was one of the few who hadn't fallen into line. So although Capone had spent St Valentine's Day in his Florida
45 mansion, there was no doubt who had killed Moran's men in that North Side garage.

Amazingly, one of the gangsters had survived the shooting. Frank Gusenberg was
50 one of Moran's top advisers. In hospital, Sergeant O'Neill begged him to reveal who had shot him. 'I'm not gonna talk,' was all he could get out of the hardened criminal.

Then, at last, Gusenberg motioned to the
55 officer. 'I'm cold,' he whispered, 'get me another blanket.' But Gusenberg was already covered with blankets. The cold he felt was the cold of death. As it swept over him, it carried away the only witness to
60 Chicago's biggest gangland massacre.

Boom

For many Americans, the 1920s were a time of great prosperity. Thousands bought a 'Tin Lizzie' – a black Model T Ford. By 1929 nine million households had a radio. Chain stores such as Woolworth's appeared in towns all over America. For those with little money, American businessmen invented 'the instalment plan'. People paid a deposit, followed by small payments each month. In 1929, President Herbert Hoover claimed that 'the poor man is vanishing from among us'. Soon, he said, there would be 'a chicken in every pot and two cars in every garage'.

Yet not all was well in the United States in the 1920s. Although America was a democracy, her political leaders were second-rate. During the Presidency of Warren Harding (1921-23), members of the government used their power to make their fortunes. His successor, Calvin Coolidge (1923-29), was a mean, tough politician.

In the north, the government seemed powerless against organised crime. In the south, the Ku Klux Klan attacked Negroes, Jews and Roman Catholics. Many farmers were poor. Most of America's black population were desperately poor. Clifford Burke, a black American who spent most of his life as a volunteer community worker, said in 1970:

The Negro was born in depression. It didn't mean too much to him, the Great American Depression, as you call it. There was no such thing. The best he could be was a janitor or a porter or shoe-shine boy. It only became official when it hit the white man.

Crash

The Depression hit the white man in 1929. Share prices on Wall Street, New York's stock exchange, collapsed. Many people were ruined. They stopped buying things. Firms went bankrupt. They laid off workers, who also stopped buying things. More firms went bankrupt. By 1932, over 12 million people were out of work – 24 per cent of the working population. Soon after, the banks started to go bankrupt. People took their money out of the banks. More banks went bankrupt.

The Great Plains of North America had been so over-cropped that during the 1930s the soil began to blow away in huge dust storms. John Steinbeck's famous novel *The Grapes of Wrath* written in 1939 tells the story of poor farmers, ruined by the 'dust bowl', who were forced to move to California.

There was no system of social security in
120 America, as there was in Europe. People
who were out of work went hungry.
Yip Harburg was one of them. In 1970,
he remembered:

I like comfort. So I went into business.
125 I thought I'd retire in a year or two. And
a thing called Collapse, bango! socked
everything out. 1929. All I had left was
a pencil.

A friend told him, 'You've got your
130 pencil. Get your rhyming dictionary and
go to work.' He did. In 1932 he wrote,
'Brother, Can You Spare a Dime?' – the
song which came to represent all those
people ruined by the depression.

135 Soon there were long 'breadlines' of
people, waiting at the charity soup
kitchens. Camps of ramshackle huts
grew up outside the towns. They were
called 'Hoovervilles', after the President
140 who could not bring the Depression to
an end. In the spring of 1932 a number
of ex-soldiers built a Hooverville in
Washington DC, the American capital.
The army had to use tear gas to force
145 the men to clear the camp.

'The country was in such a state of
confused desperation that it would have
followed almost any leader anywhere he
chose to go', wrote one journalist. That
150 was how democracy had failed in Italy
and Germany. Was America going to
go the same way?

? ? ? QUESTION ? ?

List the things that were wrong in
the United States in 1932. Was
America on the verge of revolution?

FDR

America did not get a dictator. It got
Franklin D. Roosevelt. Roosevelt had been
confined to a wheel chair since an attack   15
of polio in his twenties, but he was a man
of great power and energy.

In the presidential elections of 1932
Roosevelt promised to go to war against
the Depression. His theme music was *Happy*   16
Days are Here Again! 'I pledge myself to a
new deal for the American people,' he told
the electors.

Like Hitler, Roosevelt was a master of
propaganda. Unlike Hitler, he spoke to the   16
nation on the radio, from his front room.
Listeners could hear the fire crackle in the
background. There, 'like a father discussing
public affairs with his family in the living
room', he talked about what he wanted to do. 17

One of the first things Roosevelt did was
to end Prohibition. 'I think this would be a
good time for a beer,' he said. This
destroyed the power of the gangsters, who
could no longer make money from illegal   17
booze.

Below: 'On the breadline'. Unemployed people line
up for bread and soup during the Depression.

The 'Alphabetical Agencies' of the New Deal

WPA Works Progress Administration
Gave unemployed Americans work building schools and playgrounds. People were also employed to plant trees, and build large projects such as dams, bridges, harbours, aeroplanes and warships.

HOLC Home Owners' Loan Corporation
Gave loans to home owners who could not keep up with the mortgage payments on their houses.

TVA Tenessee Valley Authority
Built dams and factories in a depressed area using government grants.

AAA Agricultural Adjustment Administration
Gave subsidies to farmers who reduced production. This raised prices and the profitability of farming.

Social Security Law (1935)
Gave pensions to old people, and provided a small amount of unemployment benefit.

An American newspaper cartoon of 1933. Roosevelt throws out Hoover's empty promises (including the chicken in the pot). 205

The New Deal

To deal with the Depression, Roosevelt was given emergency powers for one hundred days (9 March – 16 June 1933). He became a 'democratic dictator'. His programme was called the New Deal.

Not everybody liked what Roosevelt was doing. For Hoover, Roosevelt's 'alphabetical agencies' smacked of Communism. Other politicians feared Roosevelt's power:

??? QUESTION ???

What makes the letter from the two old folks (*right*) so moving?

But for ordinary Americans, Roosevelt had saved them from poverty. They were genuinely grateful to him: 215

Dear Mr President,
This is just to tell you everything is all right now. The man you sent found our house all right and we went down the bank with him and the mortgage can go on for a while longer. You remember I wrote you about losing the furniture too. Well, your man got it back for us. I never heard of a President like you, Mr Roosevelt. Mrs _____ and I are old folks and don't amount to much, but we are joined with those millions of others in praying for you every night. God bless you, Mr Roosevelt. 220 225 230

61

BRITAIN IN THE 1930S

The Slump

The Depression of the 1930s, sometimes called the Slump, hit Britain hard. The heavy industries (coal, steel and shipbuilding) were worst hit. By 1931 nearly three million people were unemployed. Wales, Scotland and
5 the north of England became 'distressed areas'.

Many young people were angry at the poverty and unfairness. Writers such as the Welsh poet Dylan Thomas criticised the government and tried to shock their readers. In 1936, Thomas wrote a short story about an imaginary
10 Welsh village which he called *Llareggub*. Work out what it spells backwards.

Many people turned to Communism. Others, however, joined the British Union of Fascists (formed by Oswald Mosley in 1932), which was modelled on Mussolini's
15 Italian Fascists. By 1934 the BUF had 20,000 members. At huge rallies, they gave the Nazi salute and chanted 'Hail Mosley' and 'Down with the Jews!' Mosley's 'blackshirts' beat up hecklers and threw them out.

This poem rejects everything that the government does to try to improve life, and everything people do to make their life seem worthwhile – it's all 'no go'.

John MacDonald found a corpse, put it under the sofa,
Waited till it came to life and hit it with a poker.
Sold its eyes for souvenirs, sold its blood for whisky,
Kept its bones for dumb-bells to use when he was fifty . . .

It's no go the Herring Board, it's no go the Bible.
All we want is a packet of fags when our hands are idle.

It's no go the picture palace, it's no go the stadium,
It's no go the country cottage with a pot of pink geraniums.
It's no go the government grants, it's no go the elections,
Sit on your arse for fifty years and hang your hat on a pension.

extracted from **Louis MacNeice**, *Bagpipe Music*

In 1931 unemployment benefit for a family with two children was 20
£1 10s (half of what was regarded as an adequate wage for a working man). This 25
money was stopped after 26 weeks. After that, families had to apply to a Public Assistance Committee. 30
They had to take the hated 'means test' to make sure they had nothing that could be used to raise money. 35
For example, people with a piano had to sell it. Many unemployed people lost all hope. 40

The Battle of Cable Street

On 4 October 1936 the British Union of Fascists planned a march through the East End of London. The area was full of poor Jews and Communist dockers. A crowd of a quarter of a million people gathered, determined to stop the march by blocking the route. As one man remembered later:

There was a forest of banners, and one stands out in my mind. 'They Shall Not Pass.' I remember, though I didn't really understand, that this is why I had come out with my fellow Jews, that the Fascists would not pass in East London.

Most of the fighting that day occurred between the crowd and the police, who were trying to make a way for the Fascists to march. While the Fascists waited, the police first tried to force a path through the crowd. They failed. The people were too densely packed.

Next, the police tried to clear a way down Cable Street, a side road. What happened there is known as the battle of Cable Street. The inhabitants dragged furniture into the road and built barricades. They pulled up the cobblestones to use as missiles. Jews fought beside dockers. Women threw milk bottles from upstairs windows. And they won. Some policemen simply surrendered. The police could not force a way through.

Instead, the Fascists marched into the centre of London. As they went, they pasted up posters saying, 'Kill the Dirty Jews'. Next day, they returned to the East End and smashed the Jews' shop windows in the Mile End Road.

In November, the government gave the police the right to ban political marches. The battle of Cable Street marked the end of Fascism in Britain. As one historian has written:

Cable Street was one of the punctuation marks of our times, for it was there that the Londoners looked Fascism in the eye, and said No.

J Cameron, Yesterday's Witness (1979)

63

The Jarrow Crusade

Jarrow is a town in the north-east of England. Its shipyard, Palmers' of Jarrow, employed 8,000 men. But Palmers' launched its last ship in 1932. In 1934, Palmers' was closed down. Jarrow died. By 1935, 73 per cent of the working population of Jarrow were out of work. Almost fifty years later, Ritchie Calder still remembered how bad things were:

In Jarrow you saw the face of hunger in the 1930s.
You weren't seeing it on a poster.
You weren't seeing it on the telly.
You were seeing hunger in your own street, in your own mirror.

In 1936, **Ritchie Calder** *was a newspaper reporter. He was speaking during a radio broadcast in 1979.*

In 1935 the people of Jarrow elected Ellen Wilkinson to be their first Labour M.P.

'What do [the government] propose to do?' she demanded.

Walter Runciman, President of the Board of Trade, was scornful.

'Jarrow must work out its own salvation,' he said.

The people of Jarrow were furious. They decided to march to London.

2 David Riley stands on upon a small platform beneath the banner . . .
His arm is raised and says:
        I will not be broken.
His mouth is open and says:
        I will not be stopped.
His shoulders are straight and say:
        We shall not bend. . .
A small boy beneath him,
        hands on hip,
a mask lifted from his face,
        him, he too, he says so.

Tom Pickard, *Jarrow March (1982)*

1 I think we should get down to London with a couple of bombs in our pockets . . . These people do not realise that there are people living in Jarrow today under conditions which a respectable farmer would not keep pigs . . . We must do something outrageous which will make the country sit up.

David Riley, *the Marshall (organiser) of the Crusade, speaking in 1936.*

3 We decided, why not a march to London? We can show them that with all our trouble we still have a bit of spirit left.

Joe Symonds, *speaking on the radio in 1979. In 1936 he was one of the unemployed Palmers' workers.*

? ? ? ? QUESTION ? ? ? ?

Use Sources 1–5 to suggest reasons why the Jarrow marchers marched.

4 We thought we'd show our protests to the House of Commons [and] demand the right to work, which was a God given right.
Paddy Scullion, *talking to Tom Pickard in 1982. In 1936 he was a Councillor of Jarrow.*

5 The promoters of the march from Jarrow to London have now made definite arrangements for 200 marchers to take to the road on 5th October. The plans are being carried out by Miss Ellen Wilkinson MP, a former Communist.
Memo to the Metropolitan (London) Police, *1936. Police Special Branch*

6 In one family there were four volunteers from whom only one could go. And the brothers gave the trousers and the jacket and the father gave the boots and the uncle gave the raincoat. And the family marched with one man.
Ritchie Calder, *talking to Tom Pickard in 1982.*

7 Monday 5 October 1936. Well-wishers, relatives and the town band accompanied the marchers to the town boundary as they set out for London.

8 This photograph shows Ellen Wilkinson leading the Jarrow Crusade. She was a little woman, and for every stride the men took, she had to take three steps. Behind her walks Paddy the mascot dog (hidden behind two men, you can just see his legs), then come two men carrying a box with a petition in it. Behind them are a group of men playing harmonicas; the marchers sing as they walk. The newspapers called the marchers 'a walking distressed area'. Many people cried when they saw them.

9 Meal-time near Bedford. The field kitchen was loaned by the Jarrow Scouts Troop.

10 The final route was planned to go through from Jarrow, Chester-le-Street, Ferry Hill, Darlington, North Allerton, Ripon, Harrogate, Leeds, Wakefield, Barnsley, Sheffield, Chesterfield, Mansfield, Nottingham, Loughborough, Leicester, Market Harborough, Northampton, Bedford, Luton, St Albans, Edgeware and ending at Marble Arch [in London].

11 Our first stop was Chester-le-Street and we stopped in the field and our cooks made tea and dished out corned beef sandwiches . . . And I can assure you [the men] were looking forward to it . . .

But the next stop we had was at Ferry Hill, and there the miners went to town. We had a dozen chefs in white hats and everything . . .

Sam Rowan, *talking to Tom Pickard in 1982. In 1936 he was employed by Jarrow Council. His job was to prepare the way for the marchers.*

12 It wasn't an experience of misery – it was an experience of new scenes each day. New horizons, fresh air, exercise, challenge. All those things which had gone out of their lives.

Guy Waller, *talking to Tom Pickard in 1982. In 1936 he was a journalist who reported on the march.*

13 Jarrow's Crusaders are healthy in body, putting on weight, happy on the march, but their minds are troubled by rumours that the wives and children they have left behind will not receive their unemployment benefit this week.

The North Eastern Daily Gazette, *7 October 1936*

14 On Saturday 31 October, 1936, the marchers marched into the centre of London

There were two hundred fighting-fit men, they'd been marching down there, they'd been well-fed all the way down . . . Two hundred fighting-fit men marched into Hyde Park all in their Sunday best.

Sam Rowan *talking to Tom Pickard in 1982.*

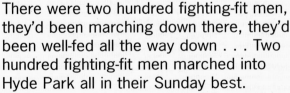

? ? ? QUESTION ? ? ?

Why did the Jarrow marchers put on weight, do you think?

15 It was a great help, the action of the boot repairers of the Leicester Co-operative Society who worked till after midnight without pay mending the boots that so badly needed repair by then. The hospital students provided by the Socialist Medical Association literally kept the men on their feet . . . Free cinema tickets from cinema managers at every town we stayed in. Kindness all the way. So many passing motorists raised their hats as we passed that we began to feel like [celebrities].

Ellen Wilkinson, *writing in The North Eastern Daily Gazette (1936)*

16 The march . . . was well organised and the men well disciplined . . . During the marchers' stay in London their conduct was perfect. No incident occurred which required police action.

Special Branch Report, *6 Nov. 1936*

17 I went back as a marcher to Jarrow. They had this special train to take them home. And we had this do . . . Oh, my golly, they did them proud. But it was very touching because the women, you see, they had to borrow. They had no clothes. They had to borrow their neighbours' clothes to come to the party.

Ritchie Calder, *talking to Tom Pickard in 1982.*

THE ROAD TO THE SECOND WORLD WAR

The Failure of the Treaty of Versailles

Hitler had promised to make Germany great again. He began to build up his armed forces. In 1935, he introduced conscription (calling men up to serve in the army). This broke the terms of the Treaty of Versailles, but Britain and France let him get away with it.

Germany was not the only great power causing concern in the 1930s. In 1931 the Japanese invaded China. The League of Nations made a protest, but the Japanese ignored it. In 1935, the League could not stop Mussolini invading Ethiopia.

On 7 March 1936, Hitler broke the Treaty of Versailles again. He sent German troops into the Rhineland. It was a bluff – Germany had only 22,000 soldiers, and they had orders to retreat if they met any resistance. But once again, Hitler got away with it. The other powers did nothing.

Hitler decided that France and Britain did not dare to stop him. He told his generals to get ready for war in four years' time. He made alliances with Japan and Italy. He sent German troops and planes to help the Fascist leader General Franco in the Spanish Civil War. Some historians believe that March 1936 was the date when the Second World War became unavoidable.

In 1934, the Nazis had failed in an attempt to take over Austria. In 1938, they tried again. First, the Austrian Nazis demanded union with Germany. Then Hitler invaded Austria. This, again, broke the Treaty of Versailles, but nobody did anything. So two months later Hitler encouraged the Nazis in Czechoslovakia to demand union with Germany, and made plans to invade Czechoslovakia.

The Failure of Appeasement

40 At this point, the British Prime Minister, Neville Chamberlain, visited Hitler. He decided that Hitler 'was a man who could be relied upon'. Hitler wanted the Sudetenland. This was the part of
45 Czechoslovakia where Germans lived. At Munich, on 29 September, France and Britain gave Hitler the Sudetenland. The Czech government was not even present at the meeting. Chamberlain's policy – giving
50 the bully what he wanted – was called 'appeasement'. It failed. Five months later, in March 1939, Hitler's troops marched into the rest of Czechoslovakia.
   Between Germany and German East
55 Prussia was the important port of Danzig and the narrow strip of land called the Polish Corridor. Hitler now demanded Danzig, and the right of way through the Polish Corridor. The Germans in Danzig
60 demanded union with Germany. Hitler threatened war.

Many historians have called the Spanish Civil War a 'dress rehearsal' for the Second World War. Hitler used
65 the Spanish Civil War to give his troops and air force (*Luftwaffe*) experience of real war. In April 1937, German bombers attacked the small Spanish town of Guernica. More than
70 1600 people were killed.

   In August 1939, Hitler made an alliance with Russia. A secret clause said that the two powers would attack Poland and divide the country between them. 'Now the West will not intervene,' said Hitler. On   75
1 September he invaded Poland.
   But Chamberlain had reached the end of his patience. In March 1931 he had promised to support the Poles if Germany attacked Poland. Now, on 3 September   80
1939, Britain declared war on Hitler. That day Chamberlain spoke to the nation on the radio:

This country is at war with Germany . . .
May God bless you all. May He defend   85
the right, for it is evil things that we shall
be fighting against – brute force, bad faith,
injustice, oppression and persecution;
and against that I am certain that right will
prevail.   90

Historians disagree about who was to blame for the war.
1 Some say that Hitler wanted war from the very beginning – one historian called the Second World War 'Hitler's personal war'.

2 Others have blamed Chamberlain for the war. They say his policy of appeasement encouraged Hitler to act aggressively.
What do you think?

THE ROAD TO WAR

1933–1938

28 March 1939
Hitler demanded Danzig and the Polish Corridor. Britain promised to support Poland and began to call up men for the army.

15 March 1939
German troops occupied the rest of Czechoslovakia. France began to re-arm.

11 March 1938
German troops occupied Austria. Hitler declared the *Anschluss* (union) with Germany.

24 November 1936
Alliance between Germany and Japan: they formed the 'Anti-Comintern Pact' against communism.

18 June 1935
Britain made an agreement with Hitler, allowing Germany to have a navy.

16 March 1935
Hitler introduced conscription and re-armed his army and air force. Britain and France let him.

30 January 1933
Hitler became Chancellor of Germany. He had said he would destroy the Treaty of Versailles and give Germany an empire.

23 August 1939
Alliance between USSR and Germany; they agreed to invade and divide Poland between them.

1 September 1939
Germany invaded Poland. Britain and France declared war on Germany on **3 September 1939.**

1 October 1938
At Munich, Britain, France and Italy gave Germany the Sudetenland. German troops marched in.

May 1938
Hitler encouraged Nazis in the Sudetenland in Czechoslovakia to demand union with Germany.

1 November 1936
Alliance between Germany and Mussolini's Italy: 'the Axis'.

July 1936
The Spanish Civil War broke out. German troops and air force helped General Franco.

7 March 1936
German troops marched into the Rhineland. Britain and France did nothing.

13 January 1935
The people of the Saar, which was taken from Germany in 1919, voted to be re-united with Germany.

July 1934
Austrian Nazis tried to take over Austria by murdering Dollfuss, the Austrian Chancellor. The attempt failed.

Appeasement

Below are six reasons why the British government pursued a policy of 'appeasement':

1 Some British people approved of Hitler's policies.

2 The British people hoped that a strong Germany would stop the growth of Russian communism.

3 Many people felt that events in Europe were not Britain's business.

4 Many people felt Britain was too weak and far away to be able to help.

5 Many British people wanted peace.

6 Many British people agreed with Hitler that the Treaty of Versailles was unfair.

? QUESTION ?

Try to match the reasons in the left hand column with the correct evidence in the right hand column. After you have made your choices, unravel the string to find the correct answers.

A "How horrible, fantastic, incredible it is that we should be digging trenches and trying on gas-masks here because of a quarrel in a far-away country between people of whom we know nothing."
The British Prime Minister, **Neville Chamberlain**, *speaking on the radio in 1938*

B "You have only to look at the map to see that nothing we could do could possibly save Czechoslovakia from being overrun by the Germans."
The British Prime Minister, **Neville Chamberlain**, *writing to his sister in March 1938.*

C "The treaties of Versailles were neither just nor wise . . . There is not a single person among the younger people who is not unhappy at the terms."
Harold Nicholson, *Diary (1919). He was in the British delegation at Versailles in 1919*

D "Hitler . . . attacked Communists, trade unionists and pacifists . . . These were the policies the British Conservative Party followed."
L C B Seaman, *Post-Victorian Britain (1966)*

E "Hitler . . . is a guarantee that Russian communism will not spread westward."
H A L Fisher, *History of Europe (1936)*

F By 1936, the *British Peace Pledge Union* had 100,000 members, who had all promised, 'Never again will I support another war.'

A famous moment. Chamberlain returns from Munich in 1938 with the 'piece of paper' he thought would mean 'peace in our time'. The British press hailed him as a national hero.

Historians have disagreed about Chamberlain's policy of appeasement.

Here are brief summaries of some of the things that have been said about appeasement:

It encouraged Hitler to think he could do anything. In this way it helped to cause the War.

It gave Hitler the advantage. He grew stronger and stronger. When war came it was against a strong Germany, in Poland – a country we could never hope to send help to.

Britain had done everything possible to keep the peace. Britons fought the Second World War with the feeling that they were in the right. This was important for the nation's morale.

It gave Britain time to re-arm. If Britain had gone to war in 1938, the Germans would have won easily.

It showed that Chamberlain had no experience of international politics. Hitler made a fool of him.

It was useless to stop a man like Hitler, who would never be satisfied in his demands.

It abandoned millions of Austrians and Czechs to the brutal Nazi terror.

It was a humiliation and a defeat for Britain.

It was a genuine attempt to keep peace made by a man who did not want to see millions of young men die needlessly.

THE SECOND WORLD WAR

The Holocaust

After 1942, the Nazis tried to exterminate the Jews. Nearly six million Jews were put to death. The Nazis called it the 'final solution' to their 'Jewish problem'.
5 Historians call it 'genocide' – an attempt to exterminate a whole race of people.

The Nazis used many ways to mass-murder the Jews, the most horrific were the 'death-camps' such as Auschwitz in Poland.
10 On arrival, those Jews who were unfit to work were sent to the 'shower rooms'. Here they were gassed with prussic acid gas, Zyklon B. Then the bodies were burned. This is why it is called 'the holocaust'.
15 The Nazis believed they were a super-race – the 'Aryans' – better than all other races. Especially, they claimed that they were better than the Jews, the blacks, and the Slav peoples of eastern Europe. The Nazis
20 took these ideas from H S Chamberlain, a British writer who had twisted the theory of evolution to 'prove' that whites were better than blacks.

As the 'master race', the Nazis claimed the right to treat 'inferior' people how they 25 wanted. They bullied, starved and tortured them. Here is just one of thousands of descriptions of life in the camps:

For days on end, a little girl sat at the bedside of her mother. The little mite was 30 dreadfully dirty, her clothes torn, her hair sticky with nits, her legs swollen by dropsy. But there she sat, forcing the dying patient to eat lukewarm bits of leather until with a greedy yet guilty glance she swallowed the 35 food herself.
The mother had pushed the blankets aside, they pressed too heavily on the swollen legs. Like white glass pillars they lay on the grey blanket which was crawling 40 with lice. The scarf which had been wrapped around the head had slid off revealing the encrusted, short-cut hair. The child cried and got up in order to find some food. 'Mother,' it said as it left. 45 'Mother, I am going to find you some soup.' The woman, who had been a famous beauty in the Jewish quarter of Amsterdam, did not reply. Her small puffed-up hand dangled from the wooden bedstead; the 50 water dripping from the open wounds on her fingers made wet stains on the soil.
When the girl returned, the mother had died. For a long time, the little mite sat on the bed. Finally the others spread the 55 blanket over the body and adjusted the headscarf. Still holding the red beaker with the soup in her hand, she left. Now she was all alone. The father had died from the fever in the camp. 60

From the diary of **Renata Laquer***, 1945*
Renata was a Dutch Jew who was sent to the Bergen-Belsen concentration camp. After the war, she went to the USA. Today, she looks after dying cancer patients. 65

The Nazis did not just massacre the Jews. They used them for medical experiments. For instance, they wanted to see the effect upon a man of removing his testicles without anaesthetic.

Some Fascist historians deny that the holocaust happened at all. That is ridiculous – there is too much evidence which proves it. However, fair-minded historians have pointed out that the Nazis were not the first people to attack the Jews. Nor was it only Jews whom the Nazis killed. They also tried to exterminate gypsies, homosexuals and other 'socially undesirable' people.

Also, throughout history, there have been other, worse examples of mass slaughter.

In fact, Stalin killed 20 million Russians during the 1930s. The holocaust has become well-known because so many of the survivors were educated people who could write about the horrors they had suffered; the illiterate Russian peasants massacred by Stalin have gone unnoticed.

After the war, the British, French, Russians and the Americans set up the Nuremberg Trials to try Nazi war criminals. It was estimated that up to 200,000 Nazis were responsible for the murder of the Jews. Only about 35,000 were ever convicted. The British sent only three investigators, and stopped all investigations in 1946.

Below and *left*: Bodies lying on the ground at the concentration camp at Bergen-Belsen. These pictures were taken by the British army on April 17 1945, two days after liberation.

? ? ? QUESTION ? ? ?

Some Nazi war criminals are still alive. Should we arrest them and put them on trial, or let the matter drop?

1 1939 Blitzkrieg
Germany (1 September) and Russia (17 September) invaded and conquered **Poland**. The German method of war was called **blitzkrieg** ('lightning war').

2 1939–40 'Sitzkrieg'
Britain sent soldiers to France. In Britain, town children were **evacuated** to country villages. Nothing else happened in western Europe; this period was called the **Phony War** (September 1939–May 1940).

3 1940 Norway
The Germans invaded **Norway** (9 April). A British attempt to help was a failure. Churchill took over as Prime Minister (10 May). On the same day, Britain founded the **Home Guard**.

4 1940 Dunkirk
The Germans invaded Holland and Belgium (10 May) and France (15 May). The Allied forces collapsed. Britain withdrew her soldiers by sea from **Dunkirk** (26 May–4 June).

20 1945 Hiroshima
The Americans captured the islands of **Iwo Jima** (19 February–17 March 1945) and **Okinawa** (1 April–21 June) from the Japanese in the Pacific. They dropped atomic bombs on **Hiroshima** (6 August) and **Nagasaki** (9 August). Japan surrendered (14 August).

19 1945 Torgau
Allied forces attacking from the west met the Russians invading Germany from the east at Torgau (23 April). The Russians **stormed Berlin**. The Italians murdered Mussolini (28 April). **Hitler committed suicide** (30 April) and Germany surrendered (7 May).

18 1945 Dresden
British and American bombers bombed Germany. They dropped 1,478 tons of high explosive and 1,182 tons of incendiaries (firebombs) on **Dresden** (13–14 February 1945), causing a firestorm. Estimates of the dead vary from 35,000 to 135,000.

17 1944 D-Day
Allied forces landed on the Normandy beaches (**D-Day**: 6 June 1944) and forced the Germans back. Hitler's opponents tried to assassinate him in a bomb plot (20 July 1944). A German counter-attack failed (**the Battle of the Bulge**, December 1944–January 1945).

16 1944 Baby Blitz
The Germans attempted another Blitz (January–March 1944), but it failed. They then, after the first V-1 rocket attack on 13 June 1944, used V-1 ('**doodlebugs**') and V-2 rockets to attack Britain.

15 1942 El Alamein
The British 8th Army defeated the Germans at **El Alamein** (October–November 1942). The British and Americans drove the Germans out of North Africa, and invaded Italy. Churchill called El Alamein the 'turning point of the war'.

5 1940 Battle of Britain Britain stood alone. The German *Luftwaffe* (air force) tried to destroy the British RAF (**the Battle of Britain**: July–September). On 15 September the RAF bombed the barges that Hitler had gathered to invade Britain.	**6 1940 The Blitz** The German *Luftwaffe* began night-bombing British cities ('**The Blitz**' September 1940–May 1941) First they bombed London for 76 nights running, then they switched their raids to other British cities, notably **Coventry** (on 14 November 1940).	**7 1940–41 North Africa** The Italians entered the war (10 June 1940). They were helped by the Germans. The British were forced out of **Greece** (April 1941) and driven back in North Africa.	**8 1941 Lend-Lease** Britain ran out of money to buy weapons. President Roosevelt of the USA passed the **Lend-Lease Act**, giving Britain all the weapons she wanted, to be paid for after the war. Under Lend-Lease, the USA supplied weapons worth $48.5 billion.

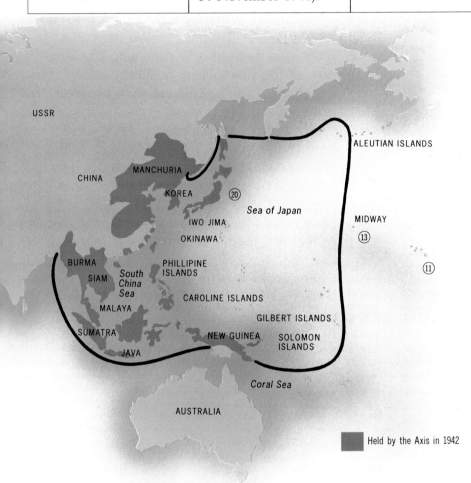

USSR

CHINA

MANCHURIA

KOREA

IWO JIMA

OKINAWA

BURMA

SIAM

South China Sea

MALAYA

SUMATRA

JAVA

PHILLIPINE ISLANDS

CAROLINE ISLANDS

NEW GUINEA

Coral Sea

AUSTRALIA

Sea of Japan

⑳

ALEUTIAN ISLANDS

MIDWAY

⑬

⑪

GILBERT ISLANDS

SOLOMON ISLANDS

Held by the Axis in 1942

9 1941 Barbarossa
Hitler invaded Russia (**Operation Barbarossa**, in June 1941). The Russians fell back until, in October, Hitler was only 60 miles from Moscow. However, the German attack ground to a halt in the freezing winter

10 1941 Atlantic Charter
German **U-boats** sank many British supply ships. Churchill signed the **Atlantic Charter** with Roosevelt (12 August 1941). They agreed to oppose the Nazis and uphold human rights. America agreed to 'shoot on sight' any U-boats.

14 1942 Stalingrad The Germans attacked Russia again and reached **Stalingrad** (August 1942). After a very fierce hand-to-hand battle, the Germans surrendered (31 January 1943). The Russians began to drive the German Army back towards Germany.	**13 1942 Midway** The Japanese captured many Pacific bases, including **Singapore** (15 February 1942). The US Navy stopped the Japanese at the **battle of Midway** (3 June 1942). Then they began to drive them back, island by island ('island-hopping').	**12 1942 Holocaust** At the Wannsee Conference (20 January 1942), the Nazis decided to put their 'final solution' into practice: to kill all the Jews at camps such as **Auschwitz**. Around six million Jews were killed.	**11 1941 Pearl Harbor** The Japanese made a surprise attack on **Pearl Harbor**, the US navy base in the Pacific (7 December 1941). The USA declared war on Japan and Germany (8 December 1941). Churchill said that this was when he realised he would win the war.

Dunkirk – the Miracle on the Beaches?

In May 1940, the Germans invaded Belgium and France. They easily defeated the Allied forces. The Belgians surrendered on 28 May. The British Army withdrew to Dunkirk. It looked as though all was lost.

'Operation Dynamo' was set up to bring the soldiers back to England. Between 26 May and 4 June, around 345,000 British, French and Belgian troops were evacuated. In Parliament, Churchill called the evacuation 'a miracle of deliverance'. And, he continued, 'there was a victory in this deliverance'.

In the cinemas, Movietone News reported the evacuation like this:

More cheering evidence of the success of this amazing military exploit is the presence in Britain of large numbers of French soldiers . . . They are showered with hospitality and find the tea of old England almost as refreshing as their familiar coffee . . .

Enjoying an unexpected seaside holiday, they bask in the sun, awaiting orders to return to France.

The story of that epic withdrawal will live in history as a glorious example of discipline [amongst our troops] . . . We passed ship after ship packed with men who the long arm of the Royal Navy had brought off the beaches of Dunkirk. Every kind of small craft – destroyers, paddle steamers, yachts, motor boats, rowing boats – have sped here to the burning ruins of Dunkirk to bring off the gallant British and French troops betrayed by the desertion of the Belgian king.

Here in these scenes off the beaches of Dunkirk you have one of the dramatic pictures of the war. Men wade to a vessel beached at low tide, its crew waiting to haul them aboard. Occasional German planes fleck the sky, but where was the German Navy? Of German sea power there was little trace.

Below: an artist's impression of the evacuation of Dunkirk.

Angus Calder is an historian of the Second World War. He believes the
British have over-glamorised the achievement of Dunkirk. He tries to 'debunk'
the 'Dunkirk myth' (to make it seem less wonderful than it was said to be).
These are summaries of some of the points he makes:

1 As early as 22 May, the British were getting
ready to evacuate their troops. They pulled back
from the fighting. This helped the Germans to
defeat the French and the Belgians.

2 The British started to take out their troops on
26 May. They did not tell the French until three
days later. While the French Army was trying to
defend Dunkirk, the British were taking out their
troops – the French held back the Germans while
the British escaped.

3 Large-scale evacuation from the beaches was
only tried on two days (30–31 May). It failed, as
the vessels got stuck on the sand. Most of the
soldiers were taken from Dunkirk port by ferries.

5 People in Britain did not
hear about the evacuation until
31 May. Then, it is true, many
small private vessels did sail
across the Channel, but only
25,000 soldiers were taken off
the beaches this way – a tiny
part of the whole number.

6 Many of the French soldiers
who were evacuated did not
like Britain. They went back to
France, where they were put
into concentration camps.

4 A few British troops
behaved badly.
• On one occasion, British
  soldiers ran away
  because of a (false)
  rumour that German
  tanks were nearby.
• Some British troops stole
  food and drink from the
  local people.
• Some officers deserted
  their troops so they
  could be evacuated first.

7 The British Army left
behind:
• 2,500 guns,
• 20,500 motor cycles,
• 64,000 other vehicles,
• 77,000 tons of ammunition,
• 416,000 tons of supplies and
• 165,000 tons of petrol.
• 68,000 soldiers were killed or
  taken prisoner.
  In private, Churchill called
Dunkirk 'the greatest military
defeat for many centuries'.

79

Living Through the Blitz

Hitler tried to bomb the British people into submission. Most of the attacks were made at night – 'the Blitz'.

Yet the air raids did not break the British people. As Winston Churchill said, 'This was their finest hour'.

This photograph shows St Paul's Cathedral in London towering over the flames. It was called 'The War's Greatest Picture'. German bombers dropped 18,800 tons of high explosive bombs on London (and 11,700 tons on other British cities). They killed 61,000 civilians.

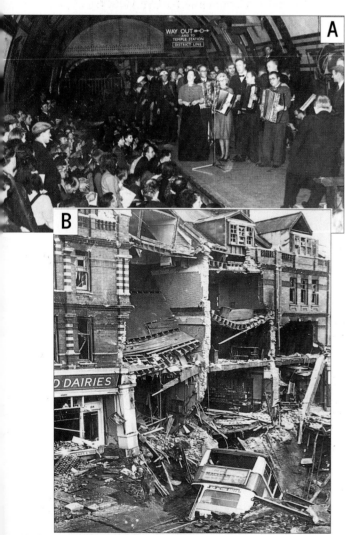

1 All reports from London are agreed that the population is seized by fear . . . The Londoners have completely lost their self-control.
Broadcast on **German-controlled French radio**, *18 September 1940*

2 What a triumph the life of these battered cities is over the worst that fire and bomb can do! . . . All are proud to be under the fire of the enemy . . . the light of glory shines upon all.

A radio broadcast by **Winston Churchill** *27 April 1941*

A In London, to escape the bombs, many people slept in the Underground railway stations stations. Sometimes, as here, they were entertained. Why might this photograph be considered propaganda?

B On 14 October 1940: a bomb killed 64 people sheltering in an Underground railway station. Suggest a reason why this photograph was not published during the war.

What did the Blitz mean to the men and women who had to endure it? These sources will help you to understand how they felt.

3 I went down into a shelter the other night . . . God, it was awful. There wasn't enough air. There wasn't enough light. And what's more important – there wasn't enough room . . . I lay on the cement, rolled my coat and tried to 'get my head down', but it was impossible. Near me there was a mother with her baby. The baby kept crying out, sometimes in a sort of whimper and then at the top of its voice. Every one was very patient about it. The mother kept apologising the whole while.

These people are brave . . .

London Air Raid Warden, *January 1941*

4 The Germans sometimes dropped incendiary bombs (fire bombs).

[Our neighbour] Mr Wright was dealing with one in his garden as another one hit his roof. The glow seemed to die down and then the tail of the bomb disappeared.

'It's gone through!' shouted Mr Wright. It had gone through to the ground floor. The bomb had burnt its way through the roof and three floors with [my father and Mr Wright] chasing after it with a stirrup pump, and Mrs Wright shrieking 'Mind my carpet' until they caught it.

The memories of **Peter Walder** *recorded in 1990. He was ten years old in 1940.*

5 [When the school was hit] it was my painful duty to help by picking up any article I saw unearthed as the men dug. I held aloft a small pink purse. No words were needed. The mother of the child to whom it belonged held out her hand, her face so anguished that it was frightful to behold. She took it and was led wordlessly away.

The memories of a **London school-teacher**, *recorded in 1971*

6 One elderly woman went to the office of the London Spitfire Fund, emptied a bag full of shillings, and said, 'For years I've been saving these to divorce my husband, but Hitler is far more wicked. You'd better have the money.'

Woman's Own magazine, *31 May 1941*

7 It was really awful, one great crash and a big flash and then there was a big fire in the shelter and I lost my mother in there, and I lost my little girl in there. We went to the hospitals – nothing there – and they said, Well, why don't you go to the mortuary? Well, naturally I went round there and he said, Well, we have one little girl here, not identified. When I looked I'd never seen such a shock in my life, all her little hair was burnt and her face where she'd put her fingers right across, all the fire was there, and I thought to myself, well, what about mother? And we never did find anything of mother.

Mrs Itzinger *of East London, describing her experiences at the time of the Blitz*

Government Propaganda

As in the First World War, the government used posters to influence people's thoughts and actions.
The posters on these pages are typical:

FACT: Expecting heavy bombing, the government organised a voluntary scheme to evacuate town children to foster homes in the counry. Many of the children who went were poor, dirty and covered with lice and fleas. Many were unhappy. Some were abused, beaten or used as cheap labour.

▽

1 'We could do with thousands more like you..'

JOIN THE

WOMEN'S LAND ARMY

△

FACT: Since Britain's farmers could not produce enough food for the population, the government recruited 90,000 girls from offices, shops and factories to be 'land girls'. They were badly paid and often over-worked, but many enjoyed the work. Male farm workers were hostile, but many farmers thought the land girls did a good job.

2 LEAVE THIS TO US SONNY — <u>YOU</u> OUGHT TO BE OUT OF LONDON

MINISTRY OF HEALTH EVACUATION SCHEME

? ? ? QUESTIONS ? ?

For posters 1 and 2, make suggestions:
1 What is the message of the poster?
2 Who is it trying to influence?
3 How is it trying to get its point across?

Many government posters were concerned with the fear of spies.

In fact, there were very few spies, and they were easily caught.

This didn't stop incidents such as the one where a woman with a strong Scottish accent was arrested and questioned by the police when she visited London!

3

4

5

The War Ends

On 24 April 1945 the Russian Army surrounded Berlin. Six days later Hitler killed himself. On 7th May 1945, Germany surrendered.

The war in the east went on for another four months. The Japanese fought fanatically. Japanese *kamikaze* (suicide) pilots flew planes packed with explosives directly into the American ships.

The Americans decided not to invade Japan. Instead, at 8.15 am on 6 August 1945, the B29 bomber *Enola Gay* dropped the first atomic bomb (nicknamed 'Little Boy') on the Japanese town of Hiroshima. On 9 August, the Americans dropped a second bomb ('Fat Man') on Nagasaki. The effects were horrific. Aircraftsman Sidney Lawrence had been captured by the Japanese, and was in a Prisoner of War camp in Nagasaki when the bomb fell. In 1994, he remembered:

The horrible part was to see the torn limbs and flesh hanging. I ended up helping the Japanese, and trying to do everything we could . . . Plutonium effects on human beings are disgusting. You've seen raw meat hanging up in a butcher's – Japanese doctors had no idea what to do with the wounds . . . We had bandages and a dark brown sort of ointment with a ghastly smell, just to soothe. I was cradling dying people or trying to put this stuff on their wounds. Some of these were the very Japanese who, a few days before, had been treating us most cruelly.

Next day, the Japanese offered to surrender.

Hiroshima after the bomb.

'Mushroom cloud' from the atom-bomb

One historian has written:

After Hiroshima and Nagasaki nothing was ever the same again. Not all historical turning points are seen as such at the time, but there can be no dispute that the use of the atomic bomb in August 1945 changed the world more dramatically than any single event before.

Chronicle of the World *(1989)*

Should the atomic bomb have been dropped? The facts and quotes on this page will help you to make up your own mind.

1 Effects of the atomic bomb

- It exploded with the force of 20,000 tons of TNT.
- The temperature in the centre of the explosion reached 300,000 centigrade; fifty times hotter than the temperature on the surface of the sun. People were vaporised. All that was left were their shadows, burned into the pavement.
- The mushroom cloud from the fireball rose to 50,000 feet.
- Fires burned in Hiroshima for three days.
- Wind swept outwards at 500 miles per hour. Almost everything within a two-mile radius was flattened.
- The Americans estimated that the atomic bombs at Hiroshima and Nagasaki killed 117,000 people.
- Japanese sources put the figures at 240,000 dead, 37,000 injured and 14,000 missing.

2 To bring the war to an end, to give peace to the world . . . at the cost of a few explosions, seemed, after all our toils and perils, a miracle . . .

The end of the Japanese war no longer depended upon the pouring in of [the Russian] armies.

Winston Churchill, *Prime Minister of Britain, describing a conversation in 1945 with President Truman of America*

3 We were talking about dealing with the people who hadn't hesitated at Pearl Harbor to make a sneak attack destroying not only ships but the lives of many American sailors.

James Byrnes, *US Secretary of State, speaking in an interview in 1965*

4 This barbarous weapon was of no real use in our war against Japan. The Japanese were already defeated and were ready to surrender . . . the scientists and others wanted to make this test because of the vast sums that had been spent . . . My own feeling was that we had adopted the moral standards of barbarians in the dark ages.

Admiral William Leahy, *Chief of Staff to the President*

THE WORLD AFTER THE WAR

The Cost of Freedom

In 1948, the Communists came to power in Czechoslovakia. For 20 years, the country was a hard-line communist state, allied to Russia.

5 Then, in January 1968, Alexander Dubcek became party leader. What followed was called the 'Prague Spring'. (Prague is the capital of Czechoslovakia.) Dubcek allowed freedom of speech and of the press. He

10 arrested the head of the secret police. The Czechs tasted freedom. Some Czechs became interested in western music and fashion. Some criticised the Soviet Union.

The Russian leaders were afraid that

15 Russia's power in eastern Europe was threatened. On 21 August 1968, Russian tanks went into Prague. The Czech leaders were arrested and sent to Moscow.

The young men and women of Prague

20 took to the streets in their thousands and sat down in front of the tanks. They waved Czech flags and chanted 'Dubcek! Dubcek!' The tanks rolled on. Nobody moved. The tanks stopped.

The young people climbed onto the tanks 25 and screamed at the Russian soldiers to leave. After three days, the Russian soldiers were so disheartened that they had to be replaced by fresh troops.

The Czechs copied Gandhi's ideas of 30 peaceful protest. They caused as much disruption as they could (see picture). They took away road signs and street names. They all called themselves Dubcek, to make it hard for the secret police to arrest them. 35

Protests continued for more than a year. When the Czech team beat Russia in the 1969 world ice-hockey championships, the Czechs held joyful celebrations in front of the Russian troops, who were still stationed 40 in Czechoslovakia.

In January 1969, a Czech student called Jan Palach sat down in the centre of Prague and set fire to himself, as a protest against the lack of freedom in 45 Czechoslovakia.

What is freedom worth to you?

The United Nations

In 1945 much of the world was in tatters. Large areas of central Europe lay in ruins. Hundreds of thousands of refugees were fleeing to the west, trying to escape the Russian Army. The world needed peace, and recovery.

As early as January 1941, President Roosevelt had suggested an organisation which would give the world just that. This organisation, he said, could be called the **United Nations**. In April 1945, at San Francisco in the United States, the representatives of 50 nations came together and signed the United Nations Charter.

Roosevelt died a fortnight before the Conference, but his widow, Eleanor Roosevelt, became chairperson of the UN commission on human rights. She was a clever diplomat. Under her guidance, in 1948, the UN agreed on a **Universal Declaration of Human Rights**. It said:

All human beings are born free and equal . . . Everyone has the right to life, liberty and personal security . . . No one shall be arrested without a reason, or imprisoned without a trial . . . Everyone has the right to take part in the government of their country . . .

The United Nations is the nations' parliament. As well as the General Assembly (the full meeting of all member nations), it has a permanent Security Council of 15 countries to deal with crises. Unlike the League of Nations, the UN can use military force to keep peace.

In addition, the UN has a number of special agencies. In 1945 the most important

The General Assembly of the United Nations.

of these was **UNRRA** – the UN Relief and Rehabilitation Agency, which gave food and clothing to those places devastated by the war. The most well-known today are the **WHO** (the World Health Organisation, which improves public health in poor countries) and **UNICEF** (the UN International Children's Emergency Fund, a children's charity).

The EEC

Another result of the Second World War was that politicians realised the need for closer co-operation between the nations of Europe. In 1948, sixteen European countries joined together in the Organisation for European Economic Co-operation (OEEC). It encouraged trade between member nations. It was so successful that in 1957 six European countries – France, West Germany, the Netherlands, Belgium, Luxembourg and Italy – joined together in the **European Economic Community** (EEC). Britain joined in 1973. By 1995, 15 countries had joined the Community; its aim is to move towards greater political unity, as well as greater economic unity in Europe.

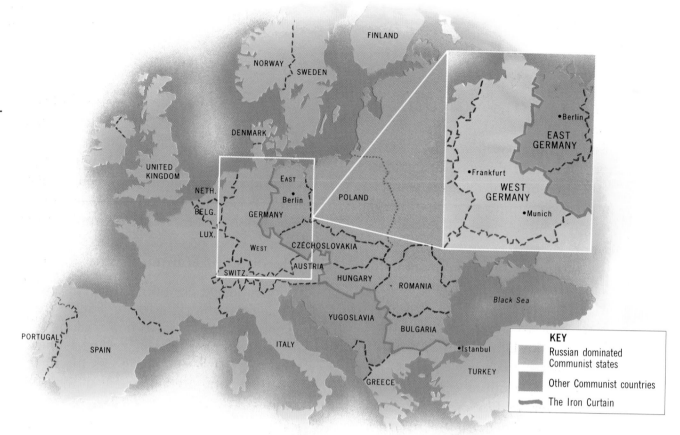

The Cold War

Russia had suffered terribly in the war. Twenty million of its people had died.
120 The Soviet leaders wanted to make sure that Russia would never be invaded again. They helped communist governments to seize power in Poland, Bulgaria, Romania, Czechoslovakia and Hungary. These coun-
125 tries fell completely under Russian control. In the words of Winston Churchill, an **Iron Curtain** came down between the communist countries of the east and the capitalist democracies of the west. In 1961,
130 the communist East German government actually built the **Berlin Wall** between East and West Berlin, to keep the two communities apart.

The leaders of the United States became
135 worried. The whole world seemed to be turning communist. So the two super powers – the USA and the USSR – became deadly enemies.

Nuclear weapons made it impossible for
140 the two sides to go to war. Both sides had enough nuclear weapons to destroy every living thing on earth many times over (**overkill**). War would destroy them both.

So both sides played the dangerous game of '**Cold War.**' First, America 145
pumped money into Europe, to stop more countries turning communist (the **Marshall Plan**). Stalin saw this as a plot to destroy Soviet influence. On April Fools' Day, 1948, he closed all road and 150
rail links to West Berlin. For over a year the **Berlin Airlift** supplied all West Berlin's needs by plane. Even though Stalin called off the blockade, in 1949 twelve western countries, led by the 155
United States, France and Britain, formed the North Atlantic Treaty Organisation (**NATO**), as a defence against communism. The Russians replied by organising their own alliance, the 160
Warsaw Pact, in 1955. Whenever one of their 'allies' showed signs of wanting to break free of Soviet control, Russian troops

marched in to restore a loyal government.
165 This happened in **Hungary** (1956) and
Czechoslovakia (1968 – see page 86).

The Americans were as aggressive as the
Russians. During the 1950s, led by Senator
McCarthy, they carried out the **McCarthy**
170 **witch-hunts** to remove communists from
every area of American life. Both the USA
and the USSR used spies to find out each
other's military secrets.

Then, in 1959, the Communist leader
175 Fidel Castro came to power in Cuba. This
was too close to the United States for the
Americans' comfort. President Kennedy
would not agree to a full-scale US invasion
of Cuba. However, in 1961, the US
180 Central Intelligence Agency (CIA) gave
weapons to some anti-Castro 'Cuban
exiles' to invade Cuba. But their invasion
at **the Bay of Pigs** was defeated.

When US spy planes discovered a Russian
185 missile base on Cuba in 1962, Kennedy
demanded that it be destroyed. The **Cuban**
missile crisis took the world to the brink
of nuclear war. In the end the Russian
leader Khruschev backed down. The world
190 breathed a sigh of relief.

The USA and communism also clashed in
the far east. The Americans developed the
'domino theory' – the idea that if one
country was allowed to turn communist,
others would fall, one after the other, like   195
a row of dominoes. In the **Korean War**
(1950-53), the United States persuaded the
United Nations to defend South Korea in
its war against communist North Korea.

When, in the 1960s, the Americans tried   200
to prop up the government of South
Vietnam, however, they became involved
in a guerrilla war they could not win.
The **Vietnam War** was a disaster for the
Americans, who were forced to withdraw   205
their forces in 1973.

One aspect of the cold war which benefited
humanity was the space race. Both sides were
determined to prove that *their* way of life was
superior. So they struggled to be the first to   210
conquer space. The Russian astronaut Yuri
Gagarin was the first man to orbit the earth
(1961). On 20 July 1969 two Americans, Neil
Armstrong and 'Buzz' Aldrin, became the first
human beings to walk on the moon. The space   215
race has had many 'spin-off' benefits, including
improved computers, Teflon (used on non-stick
pans) and 'superglue'.

Nightmare on Elm Street

On Friday, 22 November 1963, the American President, John F. Kennedy, visited Dallas in Texas. At 12.30 pm, as his car drove through Dealey Plaza, the President was killed. The impact of the shot threw him backwards and sideways.

Lee Harvey Oswald was arrested and charged with the murder. Two days later, Oswald himself was shot dead by Jack Ruby, a Dallas nightclub owner.

A Fifty-eight witnesses said they heard shots coming from the grassy knoll. The Warren Commission said they were all mistaken.

B A bullet, taken from Connally's leg and given to FBI agents, was never seen again.
A bullet taken from Kennedy's body and given to FBI agents was never seen again.
An FBI agent put into his pocket a bullet found on the pavement. It was never seen again.

C The bullet which the Warren Commission decided was the first bullet – the so-called 'magic bullet' – was found under a stretcher in the hospital to which Kennedy was taken. The pointed tip clearly showed that it had not hit anything.

D A film taken by an amateur cameraman, Abraham Zapruder, shows there were two seconds between Kennedy being hit in the throat, and Connally being wounded.

The Official Version
The Warren Report, 1964

1 Kennedy was shot by Oswald, who had acted alone.

2 Oswald fired three shots, in six seconds, using a Mannlicher-Carcano rifle, from the 6th floor of the nearby School Book Depository building.

3 The first shot went through Kennedy's neck, then through the chest of Governor Connally (seated in front of Kennedy), and then hit Connally's right wrist, before burying itself in Connally's left leg.

4 The third bullet hit Kennedy in the back of the head, and came out of the right side of the head, blowing his brains out. A 'muscle spasm' caused the President's head to jerk backwards.

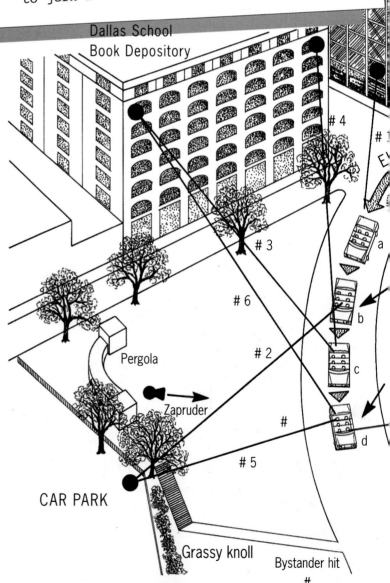

Robert J Groden (who acted as adviser on Oliver Stone's film, *JFK*) believes there were at least six shots, and at least four gunmen. He suggests:

Shot #1 missed;
Shot #2 hit Kennedy in the throat;
Shot #3 hit Governor Connally in the back;
Shot #4 hit Kennedy in the back;

Shot #5 hit Kennedy in the head; this was the shot which killed him;
Shot #6 hit Connally in the wrist.

There were perhaps four other shots (marked #).

▶● shows the position of those taking movie film of the shooting.

● shows the positions of the gunmen.

E Amateur cameraman Orville Nix had taken a film which showed the grassy knoll. He gave the original to the FBI, and a copy to a friend. The original was lost by the FBI in 1978. The copy clearly shows a gunman firing from the knoll.
  Two other privately-made films were given to the FBI. One was lost. The FBI ruined all the relevant frames in the other one.

F The Mannlicher-Carcano rifle was 'badly-made and inaccurate'. Even experts could not fire three shots from the rifle in six seconds. The gun could not be aimed properly and fired to the right. When serving in the Marines, Oswald had been a poor shot.

G Thirty two witnesses have committed suicide, been murdered, or died violently.

H The Dallas police had an audio-tape of the murder. Six shots can be heard. The tape was not made public until 1978.

I The CIA, the FBI and the US Army all refused to release all their files on the murder.

J The Warren Commission Report did not have an index. This made it difficult for anyone to check its facts.

K Before the autopsy, Kennedy's wounds were tampered with. Photographs were faked which showed the back of the head (which had been blown out) intact.

L Three men were arrested in the car park behind the 'grassy knoll'. They were later released. The police lost all their records of the arrest.

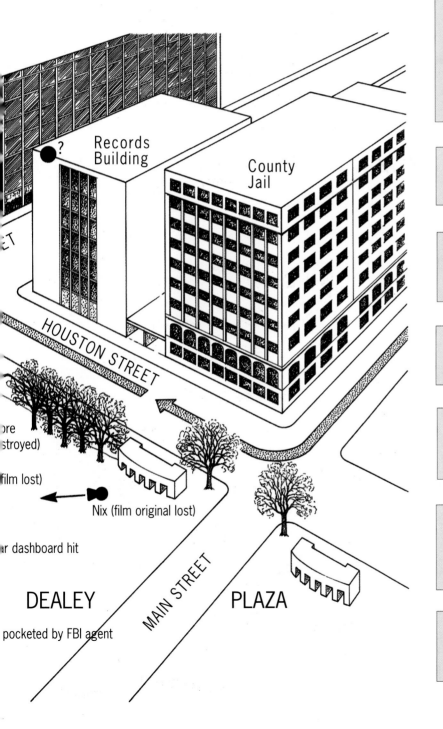

Records Building

County Jail

HOUSTON STREET

?

ore stroyed)

film lost)

Nix (film original lost)

ar dashboard hit

DEALEY

MAIN STREET

PLAZA

pocketed by FBI agent

Britain after the War

During the Second World War, the British
220 government kept up morale by promising
the people a better life after it was all over.
So, after the War, the British **Welfare
State** was set up. There was nothing like
it in the world. By 1948 it gave the British
225 people free medical care, social security
payments, free education, council houses,
employment exchanges and many other
benefits. The standard of living rose
quickly. In 1959, the Prime Minister
230 Harold Macmillan could honestly tell the

British people 'You've never had it so good'.
Unlike the United States, however, Britain
had been ruined by the war. The economy
was exhausted, and the country was heavily
in debt. After the Second World War British
industry declined. Britain became less
important as a world power. The British
attempt to keep control of the Suez Canal
during the **Suez Crisis** (1956) was a
disaster. The canal had to be handed over
to the Egyptians.

Decolonisation

It was soon realised that
Britain could no longer keep
her huge Empire. There
245 was, said Macmillan in
1960, a 'wind of change'
blowing, particularly in
Africa. Nations who had
fought against the Nazis for
250 freedom during the war
wanted to be free of their colonial
rulers. They pointed to the United
Nations Declaration of Human Rights. It said
that all people had 'the right to take part in the
255 government of their country'.

The colonial powers of Europe realised that they
would have to give their colonies independence.
In 1939 there was only one independent country in
Africa (Liberia). By 1994 *all* the countries of Africa
260 were ruled by independent, black governments
(see map, *right*). Some of these new nations
allied themselves with one of the two
superpowers. Many former British colonies,
however, joined the '**Commonwealth**'.
265 This is a loose alliance, of which Queen
Elizabeth II is the head.

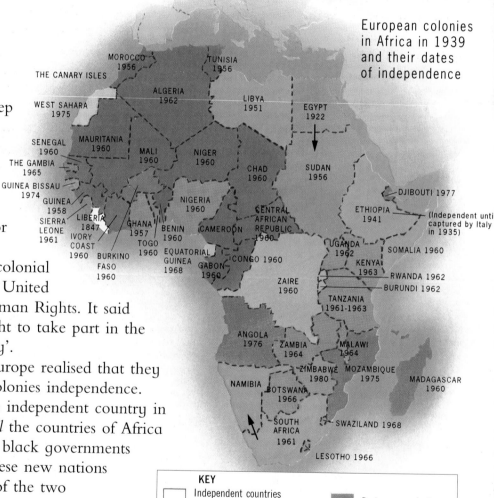

European colonies in Africa in 1939 and their dates of independence

MOROCCO 1956
TUNISIA 1956
THE CANARY ISLES
ALGERIA 1962
LIBYA 1951
EGYPT 1922
WEST SAHARA 1975
SENEGAL 1960
MAURITANIA 1960
MALI 1960
NIGER 1960
CHAD 1960
SUDAN 1956
THE GAMBIA 1965
GUINEA BISSAU 1974
GUINEA 1958
NIGERIA 1960
CENTRAL AFRICAN REPUBLIC 1960
DJIBOUTI 1977
ETHIOPIA 1941 (Independent until captured by Italy in 1935)
SIERRA LEONE 1961
LIBERIA 1847
GHANA 1957
BENIN 1960
CAMEROON
IVORY COAST 1960
TOGO 1960
EQUATORIAL GUINEA 1968
GABON 1960
CONGO 1960
UGANDA 1962
SOMALIA 1960
KENYA 1963
RWANDA 1962
BURKINO FASO 1960
BURUNDI 1962
ZAIRE 1960
TANZANIA 1961-1963
ANGOLA 1976
ZAMBIA 1964
MALAWI 1964
ZIMBABWE 1980
MOZAMBIQUE 1975
MADAGASCAR 1960
NAMIBIA
BOTSWANA 1966
SWAZILAND 1968
SOUTH AFRICA 1961
LESOTHO 1966

KEY
- Independent countries in 1939
- British colonies
- Countries with strong British ties in 1939
- French colonies
- Spanish colonies
- Portuguese colonies
- Italian colonies
- Belgian colonies
- Countries governing another country

In South Africa, a different problem developed. White people, who were only a small part of the population, would not accept an independent, democratic country. That would have meant a black government coming to power. Instead, in 1948, they set up a society based on *apartheid*. Whites and blacks were kept totally separate. The black (African) and coloured (mixed-race and Asian) South Africans were not allowed to vote. The United Nations condemned the South African government. It organised a boycott of South African goods. Apartheid did not come to an end in South Africa until 1994, when free elections were held in which everyone could vote.

Another problem area after the Second World War has been the Middle East. In 1919, the British had been given control of Palestine. After the Second World War, thousands of Jews went to live there. They wanted to set up their own state. Britain lost control of the situation, so the United Nations took over. In 1948, after a short war, the Jews set up the independent state of **Israel**. The Arab nations in the Middle East tried to destroy the state of Israel. There were more wars in 1967 (the **Six Day War**) and 1973 (the **Yom Kippur War**). The situation was made more dangerous because the Russians supported the Arabs, and the Americans supported the Israelis.

Very little of the British Empire now exists. Britain fought the Falklands War in 1982 after the tiny Falklands Islands in the South Atlantic had been captured by Argentina. Britain also still holds on to Northern Ireland, where most people want to stay part of the United Kingdom – although the IRA wish to drive the British out of Ireland altogether. There are even movements to give more freedom (called 'devolution') to Scotland and Wales.

Nelson Mandela celebrates after being sworn in as the first black South African President.

93

The Thaw

In the 1970s, after the Americans left Vietnam, relations between the superpowers began to improve. In 1972, the American
315 President, Richard Nixon, visited China. Russia and America held arms-reduction talks in 1972 (SALT I) and 1979 (SALT II). Things became less tense in the Middle East. In 1979 the American President
320 Jimmy Carter arranged a peace agreement between Israel and Egypt.

Then, to the world's amazement, in the 1980s, the cold war came to an end. In 1985, Mikhail Gorbachev became the
325 Soviet leader. He believed in *perestroika* (rebuilding) and *glasnost* (openness). He wanted major reductions in nuclear weapons as soon as possible. Then, in 1989, the USSR had free elections. The
330 result was that, for the first time since 1917, the Communist Party lost control of the government. 1989 became the 'year of revolutions'. The communists lost power in *all* the Iron Curtain countries.

The New Morality

During the 1960s, a new youth culture 33 developed in the west. Young people grew their hair long and 'dropped out'. They had more money and freedom than their parents. They went on 'Ban the Bomb' marches because they were afraid of 34
30 nuclear war. They took drugs, listened to rock 'n' roll music and had sex before marriage.

By the 1970s, their concerns had made their way into world politics. In 1972 the 345
35 Massachusetts Institute of Technology published a book called *Limits to Growth*. It said civilisation would collapse if nothing was done to reduce pollution, the population explosion, and over-use of the 350
40 world's resources. *The Brandt Report* (1980) said that the rich nations of the western world had taken so much from the poor nations of the 'third world' that the world economy was breaking down. 355
45   Today, more than ever before, people feel a need to protect the environment, reduce third world poverty and improve racial and sexual equality.

In November 1989, the Berliners 360
swarmed over the Berlin Wall and
smashed it up with pick axes and
hammers. In October 1990,
Germany became once again an
officially united country. 365

The Dream

President Lincoln abolished slavery in the United States in 1863. Yet for the next century, particularly in the southern states, most black people were treated as
70 second-class citizens. They were free, but they were not equal.

In the Second World War, black American soldiers fought for the freedom of the world. But they came home to find
375 that nothing had changed. They were were not allowed to use the same schools, the same cinema seats or the same swimming baths as the whites. In Montgomery, a town in the state of Alabama, a local law
380 said that blacks could not sit on the front seats of the buses.

On 1 December 1955, 42-year-old Mrs Rosa Parks sat at the front of the bus, and refused to move when asked. She was
385 arrested.

??? QUESTION ???

What is your dream for the future?

Montgomery was the home of Martin Luther King, a Baptist minister who believed in Gandhi's principles of peaceful protest. Black people stopped using the buses. For a year, they walked to work. 390 They won. In November 1956, the US Supreme Court declared that the bus law was illegal.

Dr King and his followers organised marches and 'sit-ins' wherever local laws 395 discriminated against blacks. They were called 'Civil Rights marchers' because they called for the same rights as the white citizens of the United States. They were often attacked, by police as well as by 400 whites, but they did not fight back.

'We shall overcome,' they sang.

On 28 August 1963 Martin Luther King spoke to 200,000 marchers in front of the Lincoln Memorial in Washington DC. As 405 the crowd cheered, he told them his dream:

I have a dream that one day this nation will rise up and live out the true meaning of its creed . . . that all men are created equal. I have a dream. 410
. . . that my four little children will one day live in a nation where they will not be judged by the color of their skin but by the content of their character. I have a dream. .
. . . So let freedom ring . . . let freedom 415 ring [and] speed up that day when ALL God's children, black men and white men, Jews and Gentiles, Protestants and Catholics, will be able to join hands and sing in the words of that old Negro 420 spiritual: 'Free at last! Free at last! Thank God Almighty! I'm free at last!'

Martin Luther King was assassinated in 1968, but his dream lives on.

Left: a peaceful black civil rights protest.

95

INDEX